AND GOD SAID,

"IT IS EASY."

AND GOD SAID,

"IT IS EASY."

How to Hear God's Voice, Have an
Intimate Relationship with God, and
Live the Abundant Life

Papa God

As Told By:

Shirley Gunter,
Stephanie Nason

XULON PRESS

Xulon Press

2301 Lucien Way #415
Maitland, FL 32751
407.339.4217
www.xulonpress.com

Printed in the United States of America.

ISBN-13: 978-1-54564-547-5

We dedicate this book to our Father God, our Lord Jesus, and our best friend Holy Spirit who love us with an extravagant love and tenderly take care of us.

Contents

Foreword
Letter from Papa God
to the Reader

A book's foreword is usually written about the author. My beloved daughters, Shirley and Stephanie, wanted to use this page to exalt Me, but I am changing things up. I desire to share what is on My heart with you, My cherished sons and daughters.

I love you unconditionally and extravagantly, My child! I desire for you to believe and trust in My everlasting love for you and your family: it is essential to fulfill your amazing destinies. My love will never fail you! The essence of My being is LOVE.

In the beginning, you were a little light inside of Me. In Me, you lived, moved, and had your being. I was the first One to hug and kiss you. I am your true Father, the Father of lights.

You are not a mistake; You are My offspring. You have been wonderfully made in My image. I called you into greatness before you were even conceived. I knit your spirit to the dot of flesh in your mother's womb.

I know everything about you, for all your days are written in My book. Fullness of joy, abundance, and a glorious future is My plan for you. My beloved child, you are My everything!

I am not the distant, angry God portrayed by religion. I am your loving Father, full of ecstatic joy and wonderful peace, who is always near you. I will always shower you with My never-ending kindness.

I love you as deeply as I love My Son, Jesus: this was demonstrated when I freely offered Him, My dearly loved and greatest treasure, as the sacrifice for you. When you receive My Son, Jesus, you receive Me. No one will ever love you or believe in you as much as I do. My never-ending love for you is beyond human understanding.

I rejoice over you with singing, for you are My treasured possession. I am a perfect Father, and I adore you with all that I am. I will never stop doing good to you, My child! It is My great desire to show you wonderful and marvelous things that you do not know. I love to bless and amaze you!

I have always been your Father and will continue to be your Father. If you seek Me, you will find Me. Delight in Me, and I will give you the desires of your heart, for it is I who gave you those desires.

My words that you are about to experience in this book will dramatically change your life if you let them. They are from the essence of My being. Will you open your heart to Me? Will you let Me live in you, with you, and through you?

I am waiting, My precious child . . .
Hugs and kisses,
Your Daddy,
Almighty God

Introduction

Be still, and know (recognize, understand)
that I am God . . .
—**Psalms 46:10 AMP**

My child, this book has been written to encourage you and to shower you with My extravagant love—a love that is easy and free to everyone who desires it! I do not wish for you to strive but to enjoy the ride! A life full of adventure and freedom is waiting for you in these pages. Are you interested? I promise that you will like what I've prepared for you.

I am a God of wonders, surprises, abundance, and splendor. Just come directly to Me for all your needs and desires. It brings Me great joy when you do, for you are My beloved. Nothing is too much to ask of Me. I am your Papa, and I love to bless you abundantly. Yes, *you!* I'm talking to you, My cherished child. Will you let Me? If so, let's go on this journey together.

The supernatural encounters you will experience while reading this book will be mind-blowing! I will jump from the pages and captivate you. You will be unable to put this book down. Lol! Supernatural healings and deliverances will spring forth as you experience Me like never before!

First, I want to introduce My two daughters, Shirley and Stephanie, who are walking out the truths revealed in this book.

Here's their story:

Both of My daughters were raised in rule-keeping, peer-pleasing religious environments, therefore lacking freedom and joy. My daughters lived for decades trying to earn My love and deserve My blessings. Striving to fill a void in their souls, they attended religious conferences, read Christian books, watched television evangelists, and listened to Christian recordings. All these endeavors to feel like they were good enough, accepted, and loved were unsuccessful; the emptiness deep in their souls was still there.

In April of 2015, My daughters, knowing there had to be more, set out on a weekend trip to a healing conference. Shirley, on a plane, and Stephanie, in a car, were traveling to the same destination unaware of each other's existence. Both were desperate for intimacy with Me.

It appeared to be another disappointing conference, but little did they know that a divine appointment had been arranged, and a friendship was kindled. My cherished daughters began to share supernatural encounters with Me, experiencing My love like never before! This intimacy with Me led to the revelations within this book.

Revelation 1:

My Sheep Hear My Voice

The Lord has appeared of old to me, saying: "Yes, I have loved you with an everlasting love; Therefore with lovingkindness I have drawn you."
—Jeremiah 31:3 NKJV

Trust GOD from the bottom of your heart; don't try to figure out everything on your own. Listen for GOD'S voice in everything you do, everywhere you go; he's the one who will keep you on track. Don't assume that you know it all. Run to GOD! Run from evil! Your body will glow with health, your very bones will vibrate with life!
—Proverbs 3:5–8 MSG

So many of My children do not understand Me because of how I'm portrayed by religion. Religion killed My Son and continues to kill My children today. Religion is demonic. I desire a world free of religion where I can have an intimate relationship with you every day. My heart longs to be involved in every area of your life, for your life matters to Me. It starts with hearing My voice.

Hearing My voice is easy! However, many of My sons and daughters do not recognize My voice. This is because most have not been taught how informal it can be: it is simply a conversation with Me like a father to his beloved child.

So turn on some soft, relaxing, instrumental music. (You can find this music on YouTube.) Close your eyes, and ask Holy Spirit to reveal truth to you. Fix your thoughts on Me by envisioning yourself (as a young child if that helps) seated beside Me in the heavenly realms or with Me and Jesus in a peaceful setting. Ask Me a question, and soon spontaneous thoughts and/or images will pop into your mind. These are from Me. Please do not brush off the promptings in your spirit or flashes to your mind, for I am answering you.

Start a journal by writing down what I reveal to you, for I have so much to share. Flow with Me and follow My leading. The visions that I give you should be reflected upon, thus enabling you to run forth in My kingdom. It's that simple; don't doubt it. I love you, My precious child. Don't doubt that, either!

When you left heaven, I opened a direct pathway or portal for you and Me to communicate. This pathway is always open and available for communication between us. I also rain down My blessings through portals. Some people call their portal an "open heaven" because it allows you direct access to Me and to heaven. I will never break this connection.

One thing that can hinder you from hearing My voice is the constriction of your portal. This can occur when you allow the enemy to put negative thoughts in your mind such as anger, resentment, fear, worries, and so on. If you feel like this has happened, search your heart to determine the blockage. Then say the repentance prayer aloud.

Let's pray:

Father, I choose to repent for participating in _____.
I loose the negative emotion of _____ from my
soul in Jesus' name. I want communication restored between
me and You, Papa. I receive your love, your peace, and your
grace in Jesus' name. Amen.

Testimony: Bill had been receiving visions of Me, Jesus, and
heaven during our intimate time together. Then, for several
mornings in a row, Bill did not see anything. Several days
before this, he had gotten frustrated with My timing. It
resulted in constriction of his portal. After the repentance
prayer was said, all communication was restored.

If you have done these simple steps and are not hearing Me,
it may be the result of an orphan spirit. The orphan spirit is
a sneaky spirit that attaches to a person who feels any sense
of abandonment. This demonic spirit can influence a person
very early, even at birth. The motive of this spirit is for you
to feel alone and unloved. It will hinder your ability to hear
Me, preventing intimacy with Me and ultimately stopping
your destiny.

If this is you, say this prayer aloud:

Father, I choose as an act of my will to loose the orphan spirit
from my soul. I forgive and release anyone who contributed
to me receiving the orphan spirit. The truth is that I am God's
beloved child. I choose to bind God's love, grace, acceptance,
peace, and joy to my soul in Jesus' name. Amen.

Romans 8:14–16 TPT
The mature children of God are those who are moved by
the impulses of the Holy Spirit. And you did not receive

the "spirit of religious duty," leading you back into the fear of never being good enough. But you have received the "Spirit of full acceptance," enfolding you into the family of God. And you will never feel orphaned, for as he rises up within us, our spirits join him in saying the words of tender affection, "Beloved Father!" For the Holy Spirit makes God's fatherhood real to us as he whispers into our innermost being, "You are God's beloved child!"

Matthew 18:18 NKJV
Assuredly, I say to you, whatever you bind on
earth will be bound in heaven, and whatever
you loose on earth will be loosed in heaven.

Testimony: Stephanie's friend John had followed the steps to hear Me several times without success. Stephanie asked Me what was blocking John's hearing. She heard, "Orphan spirit." John is from a military family, and his father was gone from home for long periods of time. So Stephanie led John in the previous prayer. John was amazed: He had his first vision upon the next soaking time. John continues to see visions and hear My voice.

Isaiah 43:4–5 NIV
Since you are precious and honored in
my sight, and because I love you . . . Do
not be afraid, for I am with you . . .

I have never quit loving you and I never will. Expect My love, peace, and grace to cascade over you as you engage in ongoing conversations with Me! As My beloved child, you have an unbelievable inheritance! In Christ, you inherit all that He is and all that He has.

Romans 8:17 TPT

And since we are his true children, we qualify to
share all his treasure, for indeed, we are heirs of
God himself. And since we are joined to Christ, we
also inherit all that he is and all that he has. We will
experience being co-glorified with him provided
that we accept his sufferings as our own.

Instructions on how we soak with the Lord:

We begin the soaking time by playing relaxing, instrumental
music from YouTube continuously. (We have discovered the
use of soft music without words enables us to hear God's
loving voice more clearly.) Our journal and pen are near us,
ready to capture the words and visions from Holy Spirit. It
is helpful to have a quiet and peaceful atmosphere with no
distractions. In the stillness, we trust that God is going to
reveal Himself like He has said in His Word.

We close our eyes and say, "Papa, we ask You to speak to us
and reveal what is on Your heart today. Holy Spirit, anoint our
eyes to see and our ears to hear You clearly. Anoint our hearts
to understand. Your Word says that when we call to You, You
answer us and show us great and mighty things which we do
not know. So we thank You in advance for revelation from
You. Most of all, we thank You for Your unconditional love
and amazing grace in Jesus' name. Amen."

As we are resting in God's love, words and images pop into
our mind. Once God starts talking to us, we write down His
words. We meditate on His exact words given for guidance
and encouragement in the days ahead. (Please remember
that it is an ongoing conversation. Papa loves it when you
interact with Him. Feel free to ask Him questions.) When
we see images, we just go with the flow. We never know

where Holy Spirit will take us. After the vision has ended, we document all the details of the encounter.

If we are soaking in a group, we allow approximately thirty minutes to receive God's words and visions. God is excited to share His heart with each one of us, so it does not take long. Everyone in the group is invited and encouraged to share their encounter. In our experience, God gives a revelation to one person and confirms or adds to the revelation through another person in the group.

As you commune with Me, I will reveal to you how to fulfill your destiny. Will you stop and listen to Holy Spirit whisper My truth into your soul? Go ahead and grab your journal now. Write down My words. I am speaking to you . . .

**Your loving Daddy, who always hears and answers you,
God**

Revelation 2:

Am I Sovereign?

The Lord isn't slow to keep his promise, as some think
of slowness, but he is patient toward you, not wanting
anyone to perish but all to change their hearts and lives.
—2 Peter 3:9 CEB

L et's look at the meaning of the word *sovereign*. The
dictionary defines *sovereign* as possessing supreme or
ultimate power; independent; possessing royal power and
status. None of these definitions mean that I, God, control
everything.

In heaven, prior to your birth, I wrote a book of abundance
and success for your life. This book details declarations
spoken over you and the destiny I have for you on this earth.
As perfectly designed as My book is for you, Satan has a plan
for you as well. He has a scheme to steal, kill and destroy My
blueprint for your life.

John 10:10 The Passion Translation
A thief has only one thing in mind—he wants to
steal, slaughter, and destroy. But I have come to

give you everything in abundance, more than you expect—life in its fullness until you overflow!

Often when life's struggles seem too difficult, My children begin to ask why God has allowed such to happen. Religion teaches that nothing can happen but what I allow. This is a false doctrine. I have not and will not cause sickness and tragedy to invade your life. That is the enemy's plan. I would never do this to teach you a lesson.

Luke 6:19 NKJV
And the whole multitude sought to touch Him, for power went out from Him and healed them all.

Satan utilizes a variety of tools to negatively influence the decisions that you make. These tools include participation in sin and unbroken generational curses passed down from the sins of ancestors. I do not allow bad things to happen to you; it is your choice to sin and/or allow generational curses to continue in your family line, thus allowing Satan to influence your mind, will, and emotions, and also to put sickness on your body.

Proverbs 18:21 MSG
Words kill, words give life; they're either poison or fruit—you choose.

I gave you a free will: the freedom to choose life or death, blessings or curses. Yes, I have supreme power, and through My Son, Jesus, I have imparted to you all My authority to overcome every power Satan possesses (see Luke 10:19). I have given you My Word as guidance to live free of sin. So the choice is yours: live a life of prosperity and success or poverty and failure.

Deuteronomy 30:19 AMP
I call heaven and earth as witnesses against you today,
that I have set before you life and death, the blessing
and the curse; therefore, you shall choose life in order
that you may live, you and your descendants.

I want someone to love and to love me back. It is never love if
you do not have a choice. I have a perfect plan for everyone's
life (see Jeremiah 29:11), but I do not make you walk this
path. For those of you who have children, do you want them
to visit you because they are made to or because they desire
and choose to spend time with you?

Roman 8:32 NKJV
He who did not spare His own Son, but
delivered Him up for us all, how shall He not
with Him also freely give us all things?

Acts 10:38 says "[H]ow God anointed Jesus of Nazareth
with the Holy Spirit and with power, who went about doing
good and healing all who were oppressed by the devil, for
God was with Him". Can you see from this verse that it was
not Me who oppressed the people with sickness, but it was
the devil?

Exodus 15:26 NKJV
[. . .] I am the Lord who heals you.

James 4:7 says, "Therefore submit to God. Resist the devil
and he will flee from you." The word *resist* means "to actively
fight against." It is My desire for you to actively fight against
all sicknesses.

Religion has taught that I am the author of your problems;
however, I only have good things in store for you. My Son,

Jesus, changed everything between Me and My children upon His death and resurrection. There is no burden to bear with Me. Jesus bore all burdens, sicknesses, and diseases so you can live an abundant life.

Luke 12:32 NKJV
Do not fear, little flock, for it is your Father's
good pleasure to give you the kingdom.

I had to deal with sin and sickness differently in the Old Testament. Now, both forgiveness of sins and healing are part of My Son's atonement. Under the new covenant, any problems in My children's lives are from your own sins, sins committed against you, and/or generational curses.

As you continue to read My revelations, supernatural healing, miracles, and encounters will spring forth! The truths presented in these pages will bring freedom like you have never experienced. It will impart to you the knowledge and the wisdom to run out religion, and to start living heaven on earth!

Psalms 103:2–3 TPT
[. . .] How could I ever forget the miracles of
kindness you've done for me? You kissed my heart
with forgiveness, in spite of all I've done. You've
healed me inside and out from every disease.

My precious child, I gave you the power to fulfill your destiny. The question is, "What will you choose?"

**Your loving Daddy, who gives abun-
dant life to all who believe,**

Almighty God

Revelation 3:

My Grace

For while the Law was given through Moses,
grace (unearned, undeserved favor and spiritual
blessing) and truth came through Jesus Christ.
—John 1:17 AMPC

But if it is by grace [God's unmerited favor], it is no longer
on the basis of works, otherwise grace is no longer
grace [it would not be a gift but a reward for works].
—Romans 11:6 AMP

N ow that you have learned to hear me clearly, let's focus on My grace. My grace is perfect for you and covers everything—all sins past, present, and future. You will squeal with delight when you let Me lead you into a whole, healed, and prosperous life—an abundant life full of My glory! In order to be led by Me, your heart must be established in My grace. So, let's begin.

Hebrews 13:8–9 AMP
Jesus Christ is [eternally changeless, always] the same
yesterday and today and forever. Do not be carried away

by diverse and strange teachings; for it is good for the heart to be established and strengthened by grace and not by foods [rules of diet and ritualistic meals], which bring no benefit or spiritual growth to those who observe them.

My grace is unearned, undeserved and unmerited; it is free to all. "How do I receive God's grace?" you ask. It is easy! Just believe. Believe that: I love you no matter what forever and always; you can't do anything to earn or to lose my love (see Jeremiah 31:3). I have loved you since you were a little light inside of Me.

Religion is the opposite of My grace. The enemy has tricked My children with religion. Religion teaches you that you need to earn My love and deserve My blessings. I tell you, My beloved child, that I desire to give wonderful gifts when you ask. I joyously give My kingdom realm with all its promises (see Luke 12:32).

Matthew 7:11 TPT
If you, imperfect as you are, know how to lovingly take care of your children and give them what's best, how much more ready is your heavenly Father to give wonderful gifts to those who ask him?

My grace is available to you as My child. Are you relying on My free grace? Remember grace came through faith in Jesus (see John 1:17). I want to shower you with My grace to heal your soul, to heal your body, and to prosper you.

Upon receiving Jesus into your spirit, you are full of My grace (undeserved, unmerited, unearned favor). In Christ, you are no longer under the religious rules or law-keeping: in Christ, there is amazing freedom! My grace will empower and

28

strengthen you in your inner man if you will simply believe that it is a free gift.

Galatians 2:19–21 MSG

What actually took place is this: I tried keeping rules and working my head off to please God, and it didn't work. So I quit being a "law man" so that I could be God's man. Christ's life showed me how and enabled me to do it. I identified myself completely with him. Indeed, I have been crucified with Christ. My ego is no longer central. It is no longer important that I appear righteous before you or have your good opinion, and I am no longer driven to impress God. Christ lives in me. The life you see me living is not "mine," but it is lived by faith in the Son of God, who loved me and gave himself for me. I am not going back on that. Is it not clear to you that to go back to that rule-keeping, peer-pleasing religion would be an abandonment of everything personal and free in my relationship with God? I refuse to do that, to repudiate God's grace. If a living relationship with God could come by rule-keeping, then Christ died unnecessarily.

When you receive My amazing grace, your desires change, and I implant within you the power and the passion to live a pure and cheerful life (see Philippians 2:13). You no longer want to sin but desire to live a life pleasing to Me. Here's the marvelous truth about living a life pleasing to Me: it is a fun way to live! I love to have fun! Heaven is profound and fun!

It is available to work for you when you rely on My Son's finished work and stop trying to do it in your own strength. Trusting in My grace means you acknowledge that in and of yourself, you are completely helpless. It is Me working in you—strengthening, energizing, and creating in you the longing and the ability to fulfill your purpose.

Galatians 3:2 MSG
Let me put this question to you: How did your new
life begin? Was it by working your heads off to please
God? Or was it by responding to God's Message to
you? Are you going to continue this craziness? For only
crazy people would think they could complete by their
own efforts what was begun by God. If you weren't
smart enough or strong enough to begin it, how do you
suppose you could perfect it? Did you go through this
whole painful learning process for nothing? It is not yet
a total loss, but it certainly will be if you keep this up!

I long for a living relationship with you, My beloved child, and
My grace made this possible. My grace knows no bounds,
and My mercy endures forever: your sins are no longer an
issue with Me. Nothing you do or fail to do can separate you
from My incredible love! Absolutely nothing!

By My grace, you have been saved. *Continue* in My grace!
Trust Me to do in you and for you what you could never do
on your own. When you believe that My grace qualifies you,
I can and will do supernatural things that will amaze and
delight you!

Ephesians 2:1–6 MSG
It wasn't so long ago that you were mired in that old
stagnant life of sin. You let the world, which doesn't
know the first thing about living, tell you how to live. You
filled your lungs with polluted unbelief, and then exhaled
disobedience. We all did it, all of us doing what we felt like
doing, when we felt like doing it, all of us in the same boat.
It's a wonder God didn't lose his temper and do away with
the whole lot of us. Instead, immense in mercy and with an
incredible love, he embraced us. He took our sin-dead lives
and made us alive in Christ. He did all this on his own, with

no help from us! Then he picked us up and set us down in highest heaven in company with Jesus, our Messiah.

You all have sinned, so embrace My grace to be forgiven. I so lavishly loved you that I sent My Son to make you righteous (put you in right standing with Me). Jesus is My free gift, My grace, to all who would believe.

Under religious laws, sin is your master. So, live under My grace—it frees you from the power of sin, and your fruit is holiness. My Son has set you free from guilt, punishment, and the power of sin! Instead of sin, offer yourselves to My ways, and the freedom never quits!

Romans 6:15–18 MSG
So, since we're out from under the old tyranny, does that mean we can live any old way we want? Since we're free in the freedom of God, can we do anything that comes to mind? Hardly. You know well enough from your own experience that there are some acts of so-called freedom that destroy freedom. Offer yourselves to sin, for instance, and it's your last free act. But offer yourselves to the ways of God and the freedom never quits. All your lives you've let sin tell you what to do. But thank God you've started listening to a new master, one whose commands set you free to live openly in his freedom!

Romans 6:22–23 MSG
But now that you've found you don't have to listen to sin tell you what to do and have discovered the delight of listening to God telling you, what a surprise! A whole, healed, put-together life right now, with more and more of life on the way! Work hard for sin your whole life and your pension is death. But God's gift is real life, eternal life, delivered by Jesus, our Master.

I want the *best* life for you—an abundant life full of freedom and excitement! Surely My goodness and mercy and unfailing love shall chase you down all of your days on earth and in heaven, and I will do superabundantly more than all that you dare ask or think (infinitely beyond your greatest prayers, hopes, or dreams) as you let My *dunamis* resurrection power work in you and for you (see Ephesians 3:20)!

Ephesians 2:7–10 MSG
Now God has us where he wants us, with all the time in this world and the next to shower grace and kindness upon us in Christ Jesus. Saving is all his idea, and all his work. All we do is trust him enough to let him do it. It's God's gift from start to finish! We don't play the major role. If we did, we'd probably go around bragging that we'd done the whole thing! No, we neither make nor save ourselves. God does both the making and saving. He creates each of us by Christ Jesus to join him in the work he does, the good work he has gotten ready for us to do . . .

My grace has been showered upon you in Christ Jesus. My grace is infinite, limitless, and free! You are forgiven by grace, healed of all diseases by grace, delivered from corruption by grace, and crowned with loving-kindness by My grace.

Romans 6:1–3 MSG
So what do we do? Keep on sinning so God can keep on forgiving? I should hope not! If we've left the country where sin is sovereign, how can we still live in our old house there? Or didn't you realize we packed up and left there for good? That is what happened in baptism. When we went under the water, we left the old country of sin behind; when we came up out of the water, we entered into the new country of grace—a new life in a new land!

Romans 6:14 ERV
Sin will not be your master, because you are not
under law. You now live under God's grace.

Let's pray:

Father, I renounce all striving to earn your love and grace. Instead, I decree that I will only do the things the Holy Spirit leads me to do. I repent for self-righteousness. I decree that I am your righteous child because of Jesus, and not my works. I receive your grace to free me from sin, to heal me, and to prosper me abundantly. Thank you for your super abounding grace and unfailing love in me and upon me right now in Jesus' name. Amen.

Your loving Daddy, who gives you grace abundantly,

God

Revelation 4:

Your Identity

But you are a chosen race, a royal priesthood, a consecrated nation, a [special] people for God's own possession, so that you may proclaim the excellencies [the wonderful deeds and virtues and perfections] of Him who called you out of darkness into His marvelous light.
—1 Peter 2:9 AMP

By living in God, love has been brought to its full expression in us so that we may fearlessly face the day of judgment, because all that Jesus now is, so are we in this world.
—1 John 4:17 TPT

Do you ever wonder what I see when I look at you, My child? Wonder, beauty, My masterpiece—you are gorgeous to Me. The apple of My eye. Royalty—My little princess, My valiant prince, My treasure, and My joy. The pleasure that comes to My heart when you see Me as your Father and see yourself as My beloved child is overwhelming to Me! You ravish My heart with one look of your eyes. O My love, you are altogether beautiful and fair. There is no flaw nor blemish in you (see Song of Solomon 4).

Not only are you My child, but once you have received My Son, Jesus Christ, you are righteous; your sins are forgiven and erased; you are free from guilt and shame; you are accepted back into heaven. My Son's one sacrifice was enough to take away all your sins forever (see Hebrews 10:12).

There was a divine exchange in which Jesus who knew no sin became sin on your behalf, so that in Him you became righteous (see 2 Corinthians 5:21). Believe in your righteousness in Christ; otherwise, for you, My Son's death was in vain.

When you know that you are My beloved, righteous child, you will come boldly to My throne of grace to find help, love, peace, guidance, provision: everything you ever want or need. Trusting in the finished work of Jesus, you can come to Me without shame or guilt. Having the revelation of My thoughts toward you, you will desire to visit Me often, and you are invited to come up here and sit in my lap. I desire to be with you always.

The more you visit with Me, the more I can share with you the plans for your future. I am love, and I choose life for you: an eternally abundant life full of blessings, joy, peace, riches, grace, and greatest of all, My love! Your destiny is full of love, power and greatness: all of which I placed in you. Will you let them shine forth?

I want you, My beloved child, to identify with My Son, Jesus. As He is righteous, pure, holy, accepted, loved, blessed, rich, and healthy right now, so are you. Refer to My Word in 1 John 4:17 for confirmation.

Don't get into self-effort to receive My love. Rest in My *love* for you, My precious child. You are My heir and a joint heir with Jesus. I will never give up on you!

I invite you now to come away with Me, and allow yourself to sink into the awareness of how deeply loved and cared for you are by Me. I want to saturate you with My extravagant and unconditional love . . .

Your Daddy, who is your identity,

God

Revelation 5:

Stepping Out into Your Identity

[. . .] I know what I am doing. I have it all planned
out—plans to take care of you, not abandon you,
plans to give you the future you hope for.
—Jeremiah 29:10–11 MSG

To some, this could be the scariest part, but that is far from the truth. It is a fun-filled, adventurous journey with Me; I promise to always amaze you. I enjoy making the adventures interesting. It's all about fun with Me and being who I created you to be.

The fun has only just begun. I have fun planning things for you, and I get excited about your future. I delight in watching you walk out My plans. I am revealing to you the ways of heaven.

You may be asking, "How does this happen?" It is through intimacy with Me. Let's expand on Revelation 1.

Intimacy is the key foundation in which I can download to you My plans, My thoughts, My desires for your destiny, My strength, My wisdom, My grace for abundant life, My healing power, My glory, and My riches. Come to Me daily. I want you to see your worth and to experience My love.

I desire to lavish My blessings on you. I will direct your path.

Colossians 1:27 NKJV
To them God willed to make known what are the riches of the glory of this mystery among the Gentiles: which is Christ in you, the hope of glory.

Come to the throne and soak in My presence. Quiet yourself down by putting on some relaxing music, fixing your eyes on your loving Lord Jesus, tuning into the spontaneous thoughts or images that pop into your mind, and writing them down.

When you come away with Me in this simple way, you will know My heart and My thoughts. Our relationship will blossom. Dynamic and intimate, you and I will be.

Psalm 37:4 NKJV
Delight yourself in the LORD, And He shall give you the desires of your heart.

I need to caution you here with the most important key in making sure it is Me and not the enemy: you must fix your eyes on Jesus, not the problem you are facing or on any person.

"What do you mean by fixing my eyes on Jesus?" you ask. Visualize yourself with Jesus, who loves you unconditionally and lavishly. Also, remember that Jesus is not sin-conscious. All your sins were washed away with His blood, when you accepted Him in your heart, and I do not remember your sins and evil deeds any longer. (See Hebrews 10:17.)

Colossians 2:10 NKJV
And you are complete in Him, who is the
head of all principality and power.

Jesus made you royalty. I want to see you *reign* on earth in this kingdom age. You are more than a conqueror through Christ who loves you. I have given you power over the enemy!

Romans 5:17 NKJV
For if by the one man's offense death reigned
through the one, much more those who receive
abundance of grace and of the gift of righteousness
will reign in life through the One, Jesus Christ.

Romans 8:37 NKJV
Yet in all these things we are more than con-
querors through Him who loved us.

Will you choose to rule and reign with Me in this kingdom age? Are you interested in knowing what I wrote about you in the pages of your book in heaven? Ask Me. I am delighted to read it to you, My child . . .

Your All-Powerful Daddy,

God

Revelation 6:

My Love

The one who does not love has not become
acquainted with God [does not and never did know
Him], for God is love. [He is the originator of love,
and it is an enduring attribute of His nature.]
—1 John 4:8 AMP

Yes, God loved the world so much that he gave
his only Son, so that everyone who believes in
him would not be lost but have eternal life.
—John 3:16 ERV

How do you understand and comprehend My love?
Let's look at 1 Corinthians 13 in a fresh, new way
today. People have looked at it religiously which was never
my intent. This is how I want you to know Me:

1 Corinthians 13 (ERV)
I am patient and kind. I am not jealous, nor do I
brag. I am not proud. I am not rude or selfish, and
I cannot be made angry easily. I do not remember
wrongs done against Me. I am never happy when

others do wrong, but I am always happy with the truth. I never give up on people. I never stop trusting, never lose hope, and never quit. I will never end.

There is nothing you could ever do that would stop Me from loving you, My precious child. It is My love who created you, because I wanted someone to share My life with.

Acts 17:26–28 TPT
From one man, Adam, he made every man and woman and every race of humanity, and he spread us over all the earth. He sets the boundaries of people and nations, determining their appointed times in history. He has done this so that every person would long for God, feel their way to him, and find him—for he is the God who is easy to discover! It is through him that we live and function and have our identity; just as your own poets have said, 'Our lineage comes from him.'

Let Me elaborate on this. Before you came to earth, you lived inside of Me and played in the river of life. I sang songs over you, told you stories, and spoke life into your destiny which is recorded in your heavenly book. You are My sons and daughters.

Nothing can separate you from My love—not death, life, angels, nothing now, nothing in the future, no powers, nothing in the whole created world! (Romans 8:38) I will never leave you nor forsake you because I love you dearly. I will never disappoint you. I want to provide for you and bless you lavishly! I adore you with all My heart.

Hebrews 13:5 AMP
[. . .] for He [God] Himself has said, I will not in any way fail you nor give you up nor leave you without

support. [I will] not, [I will] not, [I will] not in any degree leave you helpless nor forsake nor let [you] down (relax My hold on you)! [Assuredly not!]

1 John 4:19 AMP
We love, because He *first loved* us.

Remember to receive My love first. Just say, "Papa, I thank You for loving me", and I will saturate you with My love. I desire to pull you close and whisper words of life, identity, and encouragement to you, My treasured one. After you receive My love, you will then love Me back and love others with the love I first gave you.

I am showering you with My love right now as you read this. My arms are waiting to hold you . . . Can you feel My Presence? As you continue communing with Me, expect a manifestation of My Presence, and you will sense My nearness because I am real!

Hugs and kisses,

Your Loving Daddy

Revelation 7:

Salvation Is the Great Escape from a Place called Hell

For this is how much God loved the world—he gave his one and only, unique Son as a gift. So now everyone who believes in him will never perish but experience everlasting life. God did not send his Son into the world to judge and condemn the world, but to be its Savior and rescue it!
—John 3:16–17 TPT

Many of My children are being taught hell is not real. Hell is most certainly real as its creation was for Satan and the fallen angels. Hell was not intended for My children, but due to sin and unacceptance of My Son, Jesus, it becomes eternity for many.

I do not want anyone to go to hell. However, My will for the salvation of My children is not being accomplished. My Son, Jesus, paid for the sins of the whole world, but you must choose to put your faith in My Son to receive salvation. Sinners choose hell by not choosing My Son as their Savior. It is My heart for My children to be with Me in heaven. My

Son, Jesus, created the way for My children to avoid hell. What will your choice be?

John 14:6 AMP
Jesus said to him, "I am the [only] Way [to God] and the [real] Truth and the [real] Life; no one comes to the Father but through Me.

I don't care what sins you have committed. No sin is greater than the blood that My Son shed on the cross for you. My Son, Jesus, forgives *all* your sins, every single one. The blood covers all sins, iniquities, generational curses, sicknesses, and diseases.

His blood is powerful. My Son's blood is powerful enough to take care of everything when you invite him to wash away all your sins. Jesus paid it *all*!

If you would like to come back home to heaven and to Me, your Father, please pray this salvation prayer to receive all that Jesus has done for you:

Let's pray:

Lord Jesus, thank You for your passionate love for me, so extravagant that you chose to die in my place while I was still a slave to sin. Thank You for the divine exchange in which You became my sin and I became righteous. Your precious blood washes me clean of every sin. I invite you to be My Lord and My Savior now and forever. I receive Your unfailing love and grace. Because of Your finished work, heaven is now my home. Amen

2 Corinthians 5:21 ERV
Christ had no sin, but God made him become sin so that in Christ we could be right with God.

Now that you are saved and made righteous, receive My grace every day to empower you to sin no more. Don't rely on your self-efforts. Rely on the finished work of Jesus: My grace is enough. As you depend on My grace, you end up sinning less and less.

If you died still engaging in sins that My Son so bountifully took away from you on the cross, I would still love you and receive you into heaven. We can never be separated. Jesus' blood is that powerful; nothing can break our bond.

Colossians 1:13–14 ERV
God made us free from the power of darkness.
And he brought us into the kingdom of his dear
Son. The Son paid the price to make us free.
In him we have forgiveness of our sins.

After you have accepted Jesus as your Lord and Savior, you are in the kingdom of My love forever. Your good works did not get you into My kingdom, and your bad works cannot get you out. Jesus' blood made you righteous (in right standing) with Me forever.

I am not saying that you can freely sin; there are consequences to sinning. Satan can wreak havoc in your life and family when you sin. Therefore, receive My grace (undeserved, unearned, unmerited favor) daily to empower you to sin no more. Then you will live the abundant life that Jesus died to give you, My precious one.

Welcome to the kingdom of My love!

Your Daddy,

Almighty God

Revelation 8:

Please Don't Be Religious

This is all I want to ask of you: did you receive the [Holy] Spirit as the result of obeying [the requirements of] the Law, or was it the result of hearing [the message of salvation and] with faith [believing it]? Are you so foolish and senseless? Having begun [your new life by faith] with the Spirit, are you now being perfected and reaching spiritual maturity by the flesh [that is, by your own works and efforts to keep the Law]?
—Galatians 3:2–3 AMP

Many of you have been led astray in the church. My Son did not come to bring religion. He did not come to judge and condemn the world, but to save. I sent My Son, Jesus, to the earth to provide the way for you to come back to heaven (your home) and to Me. The one who believes and trusts in My Son is not judged. Read the following verse:

John 3:18 AMP
Whoever believes and has decided to trust in Him [as personal Savior and Lord] is not judged [for this one, there is no judgment, no rejection, no condemnation]; but the

one who does not believe [and has decided to reject Him as personal Savior and Lord] is judged already [that one has been convicted and sentenced], because he has not believed and trusted in the name of the [One and] only begotten Son of God [the One who is truly unique, and only One of His kind, the One who alone can save him].

My church is full of religion, causing lack of relationship with Me. I desire relationship with you, My child: a close friendship like no other, an intimacy that you can always rely on. I am your best friend, and I will always be in your corner with no condemnation.

How would you like to experience freedom, maybe for the first time in your life: no chores, no tasks, and no "To Do List"? Religion is about man doing. Relationship is about accepting the finished works of Jesus. Religion gives you a job to do, but I require no works.

Here's an example of a religious task to try to get Me to move on your behalf: fasting. See below My thoughts on this.

During a time of soaking together and preparing for this book, Stephanie asked Me about fasting. Shirley, unaware of this question, was given My answer. To their amazement, these are My words I gave Shirley to write down:

"Where's the beef? Strong meat belongs to mature believers. You two are getting more than milk. You're getting the pizza and the ice cream, too, if that is what you want. No fasting from food for My kids during the kingdom age. There is no fasting in heaven. Lol! My kingdom come, My will be done on earth as it is in heaven. Fasting from food is no longer needed, but I will honor it if you choose to . . . More and more revelations, and the higher and higher the team goes!

Rest in My glory. Have fun in My glory! Fun times are in the glory time!"

You don't need to fast from food. However, I would like you to fast from all negativity, for you do not want to give the enemy an inroad into your life. If you let My heart change the way you think and the words you speak, peace and joy will be yours!

Law is about you working for Me. Grace is about Me working for you. Jesus came not to be served, but to serve (see Matthew 20:28). Every day, you can be in a place where you "think" you are working for Me or you can believe this: whatever I need, even to serve God with, My Papa God supplies; whatever the circumstance I face, God supplies me His courage, His wisdom, His strength, and His favor. If you will wake up and realize that I am working in you, for you, and through you, you will become carefree and excited about your future!

It is by My free grace that you partake of abundant life through your faith. This is not received by your own doing or your own striving, but it is My gift (see Ephesians 2:8). When you enter through faith in Jesus, you will find yourself standing out in the wide-open spaces of My grace and glory. See the verses below.

Romans 5:1–2 MSG
By entering through faith into what God has always wanted to do for us—set us right with him, make us fit for him—we have it all together with God because of our Master Jesus. And that's not all: We throw open our doors to God and discover at the same moment that he has already thrown open his door to us. We find ourselves standing where we always hoped we

might stand—out in the wide open spaces of God's
grace and glory, standing tall and shouting our praise.

Ephesians 2:7–10 MSG

Now God has us where he wants us, with all the time in
this world and the next to shower grace and kindness upon
us in Christ Jesus. Saving is all his idea, and all his work.
All we do is trust him enough to let him do it. It's God's
gift from start to finish! We don't play the major role. If
we did, we'd probably go around bragging that we'd done
the whole thing! No, we neither make nor save ourselves.
God does both the making and saving. He creates each
of us by Christ Jesus to join him in the work he does,
the good work he has gotten ready for us to do . . .

2 Corinthians 5:19 NLT

For God was in Christ, reconciling the world to himself,
no longer counting people's sins against them . . .

1 John 4:16 NLT

We know how much God loves us, and
we have put our trust in his love.

I want you to put your trust in My unconditional love for you:
not in your works or self-effort! When you believe in your
own righteousness, Satan will use this lie as an inroad for the
religious spirit to attach and wrap itself around you, bringing
confusion and deception. In the spirit realm, this demonic
spirit manifests as a snake. Remember that Jesus called the
religious Pharisees "a brood of vipers." See the verses below.

Matthew 3:7 NKJV

But when he saw many of the Pharisees and Sadducees
coming to his baptism, he said to them, "Brood of vipers!
Who warned you to flee from the wrath to come?

Matthew 12:34 NKJV
Brood of vipers! How can you, being evil,
speak good things? For out of the abundance of the heart the mouth speaks.

Let Me help you get rid of the religious spirit. This spirit influences most of My children's minds, wills, and emotions, and they are not even aware of it.

Let's pray:

Father, I repent for trusting in my works instead of Your grace. I confess this as unbelief. Forgive me for allowing the religious spirit to dominate my thinking and influencing me to be judgmental and critical of your children. Jesus, I ask You to wash me and my family line all the way back to Adam afresh with Your cleansing blood. Thank You for the power of your blood, purifying my soul from religious strongholds right now. I call forth the fire of God to flood me now and burn up all religious snakes. Burn and be thrown into a dry place to not return in Jesus' name. Amen.

You are now free from the bondage of religion. Enjoy your new-found freedom!

**Your loving Daddy, who releases over-
flowing grace and peace to you,**

Almighty God

Revelation 9:

Intimate Relationship with Me, Your Daddy

For you [who are born-again have been reborn from above—spiritually transformed, renewed, sanctified and] are all children of God [set apart for His purpose with full rights and privileges] through faith in Christ Jesus.
—Galatians 3:26 AMP

So now we come freely and boldly to where love is enthroned, to receive mercy's kiss and discover the grace we urgently need to strengthen us in our time of weakness.
—Hebrews 4:16 TPT

The first step in having an intimate relationship with Me is to believe that My Son, Jesus, made this possible for you. His shed blood makes you righteous (in right-standing with Me). Upon your salvation, He washes away all your sins as far as the east is from the west with His powerful blood (see Psalms 103:12). After your acceptance of Jesus, you can access me sin-free, unashamed, and not guilty.

When I look at you, I see you as My beloved child, who has every right to come before Me. I desire for you to walk with Me as Adam and Eve did in the garden. Come and have fun with Me! It brings Me such delight when I hear you talking to Me. I run to hear your voice. You are My dream!

I will do marvelous things for you when you ask Me. When you share your thoughts with Me, please know that I hear you. Oh, how I long to spend time with you! I love you. You are the apple of My eye. In our precious time together, I can reveal My plans for your destiny: an amazing future of your dreams. Will you share your day with Me?

Matthew 7:11 ERV
You people are so bad, but you still know how to give good things to your children. So surely your heavenly Father will give good things to those who ask him.

James 1:17 NKJV
Every good gift and every perfect gift is from above, and comes down from the Father of lights, with whom there is no variation or shadow of turning.

My daughters will now explain to you how easy it is to access Me. I have taught them through the Holy Spirit, and I will teach you as you read My Words. So, please continue on.

Stephanie's testimony:

On the morning of November 16, 2016, I went to my quiet place, and I turned on worship music. I began worshiping God for who He is, and I imagined myself dancing with Jesus in my bedroom. I was physically dancing and singing. After three songs, I was taken up to the throne room in heaven. My Father was smiling as He watched Jesus and me dancing gracefully throughout the massive throne room. Wow! The truth is that I cannot dance.

Then, I physically sat down on my bed. My eyes were closed, and the encounter continued. When the song "Good, Good Father" ended, I ran over and jumped into Father's lap. Reaching out to hug me, He said, "I love it when you dance." Father began revealing His amazing plans for my destiny, and the encounter ended with Him saying, "Spend time with Me daily."

Shirley's testimony:

I want to begin by saying that I do not have many memories of my childhood, and before I became aware of the truths in this book, I did not understand the reason. I discovered the answer in the spring of 2017 at a Healing Hearts group while listening to a teaching on inner healing.

When I closed my eyes, trying to picture Jesus as the video taught, I realized that I couldn't see anything except the back of my eyelids. The video explained that some people will subconsciously make an inner vow to deal with a traumatic event. This resonated with me. Wow! Memories of being sexually abused by a sitter at the age of five came back to me.

I now knew the reason: an inner vow made as a child resulted in the blockage of my memory and the inability to see images in my mind. Upon this knowledge, I renounced the inner vow through prayer (see Revelation 13).

Not wanting anything to affect my intimacy with God, I asked Him for more revelation on this. Then, while my husband and I were soaking in His Presence, Holy Spirit gave my husband a vision: Jesus was taking my little hand immediately after the traumatic event and leading me to a safe and beautiful place. My husband could see that Jesus was very sad due to the offender's actions that were made against me, God's innocent and cherished child. (God doesn't override a person's free will.) Through this encounter with Jesus (feeling His loving heart and hearing His healing words spoken through my husband), the trauma no longer affects me.

A second thing affecting my ability to form a picture in my mind and thus my intimacy with God was religious teaching. I believed that all daydreaming was a waste of time, not real, and not spiritual. Therefore, I repented of believing the lies of the enemy, and replaced them with the truth: God uses our imagination to bring forth the plans and destiny He has for us.

After learning these truths, my experiences with God have deepened. I not only hear His voice, but now I receive visions, God dreams, His plans, angelic visitations, and supernatural encounters.

A Summary

Now that you have heard My daughter's testimonies to inspire you to have intimacy with Me, below is a review of the steps:

1. Believe that I want intimacy with you.

2. Make yourself available by going to your quiet place and putting on some soft music.

3. Invite Me to speak to you, imagining yourself with Me and focusing on My goodness and love towards you.

4. Be still and listen.

5. Write down the words and/or the vision so you can remember our time together. I will amaze you with the revelations you will receive!

Song of Songs 1:15 TPT
Look at you, my dearest darling, you are
so lovely! You are beauty itself to me. Your
passionate eyes are like gentle doves.

Your loving Daddy forever,

God

Revelation 10:

Forgiveness is the Key to Freedom from the Enemy

> Don't be angry with each other but forgive each other. If you feel someone has wronged you, forgive them. Forgive others because the Lord forgave you.
> **—Colossians 3:13 ERV**

Unforgiveness is a landing strip for the enemy to invade and control your mind, will, and emotions. It is an open door for sicknesses, diseases, mental conditions, and destruction. If not repented of, it can pass to future generations, repeating the same cycles.

I said, in Ephesians 4:32, to forgive one another, just as I in Christ forgave you. The reason I said this was for your protection from the enemy and your wholeness. It was not to give you an order. Unforgiveness gives the devil legal right to oppress you. I want you free from his clutches. This is a major key to your freedom and to an abundant life.

Let Me lead you in a prayer for unforgiveness:

Father, I forgive_____ for hurting me and sinning against me. Because you have forgiven me of all my sins, I make the decision to forgive _____ now. I forgive myself for participating in the sin. Thank You, Lord, for your forgiveness. I give you all the negative feelings that I carry toward _____. Thank You, Jesus, for washing all my sins away with your precious blood. I repent for carrying unforgiveness and the negative emotions that accompanies it. I receive Your love and forgiveness in Jesus' name. Amen.

Your forgiving Daddy,

God

Revelation 11:

Generational Curses

GOD, slow to get angry and huge in loyal love, forgiving iniquity and rebellion and sin; Still, never just white-washing sin. But extending the fallout of parents' sins to children into the third, even the fourth generation.
—Numbers 14:18 MSG

Christ redeemed us from that self-defeating, cursed life by absorbing it completely into himself. Do you remember the Scripture that says, "Cursed is everyone who hangs on a tree"? That is what happened when Jesus was nailed to the cross: He became a curse, and at the same time dissolved the curse. And now, because of that, the air is cleared, and we can see that Abraham's blessing is present and available for non-Jews, too. We are all able to receive God's life, his Spirit, in and with us by believing—just the way Abraham received it.
—Galatians 3:13–14 MSG

The generational curse is something that cannot be ignored. The sins of your ancestors can be passed down to the descendants if not dealt with. Satan has used this open door to destroy the families of My children for years. Marriages have been destroyed, and people have died prematurely. I want this to stop! If the curse is not broken, it will affect your emotions, will, and choices.

To break curses, pray this:

I repent of the sin of my ancestors and my own sin of _____. I forgive my ancestors for passing on to me this sin and the resulting curse of_____. I forgive myself for taking part in this sin. I place the blood of Jesus between me and my ancestors, as a baby in my mother's womb. I command the sin of _____ and all curses to stop at the cross of Jesus, and I receive freedom by the blood of Jesus.

Now that the curses have been broken and the air is cleared, let us decree this: Thank You, Jesus, for redeeming me and my family from all curses by your powerful blood. I decree that my family is now blessed with the blessings of Abraham. Our youth is renewed! We are as prosperous and successful as Abraham!

Your Daddy, who redeems you,

Almighty God

Testimony:

On August 8, 2018 (a few days before submitting this book to the publishing company), Stephanie was making decrees and breaking generational curses while driving to work. She suddenly found herself in a vision.

In the vision, Stephanie was standing in front of her parents. She could see a cord between her and each of her parents. The blood of Jesus came down and severed the two cords. Then Stephanie was flooded with the light of Jesus.

Next, Papa said to her, "See how easy it is! It is that easy to break generational curses! I will still honor the old way, but there is an easier way."

Revelation 12:

Ungodly Soul Ties

> Do not be so deceived and misled! Evil compan-
> ionships (communion, associations) corrupt and
> deprave good manners and morals and character.
> **—1 Corinthians 15:33 AMPC**

Beloved, I want your soul whole. Remember I said in 3 John 1:2 that I want you to prosper and be in health, just as your soul prospers.

I have the details and the relationships of your life planned before you leave heaven. This plan is perfect. However, the enemy will bring people into your path and create distrac-tions to divert the plan if you let him. It is up to you to choose your spouse and your friends wisely. I will not go against your free will.

Soul ties are created whenever you give a part of yourself (a layer of your soul) willingly or unaware to a person or a group. You form a soul tie with anyone, any group, or mindset that you are in a close or committed relationship with including pastors, employers, friends, children, political associations, pornography, strict theological doctrines, and so on.

Proverbs 27:12 AMP
A prudent man sees evil and hides himself and avoids it,
But the naïve [who are easily misled] continue on and
are punished [by suffering the consequences of sin].

Soul ties are like spiritual cords in which energy flows back and forth whether it be positive or negative. If you are dealing with a negative emotion such as anger or hopelessness, it could be coming from an ungodly soul tie. If violence, fear, or abuse become a part of the soul tie, it is ungodly. Domination and manipulation by a pastor or spouse is also evidence of an ungodly soul tie.

Death does not sever a soul tie. If you are experiencing negative emotions regarding a deceased person, pray to sever the ungodly soul tie. The enemy has an entrance and will continue to influence your thoughts, emotions, and decisions.

1 Corinthians 6:16–18 TPT
Aren't you aware of the fact that when anyone sleeps with
a prostitute he becomes a part of her, and she becomes
a part of him? For it has been declared: The two become
a single body. But the one who joins himself to the Lord
is mingled into one spirit with him. This is why you must
keep running away from sexual immorality. For every
other sin a person commits is external to the body, but
immorality involves sinning against your own body.

For those of you that are in a marriage with a controlling or angry spouse, you need to cut the ungodly soul tie. It doesn't necessarily mean that you end the marriage. It means you cut off the negative part of the relationship so that the spirit of anger or control doesn't enter your soul.

Making decrees over your life and relationships (see Revelation 16) and saying the following prayer allows Me to work mightily on your behalf. Come to Me, and I will reveal the negative emotion in your heart and its root cause. The root cause of negative emotions could be generational curses, ungodly soul ties, wrong beliefs, inner vows, trauma, and word curses. Once you are aware of the root cause, I will teach you how to get your soul clean and whole.

To sever the ungodly soul ties, repeat after Me:

Lord, I repent of my sin of an ungodly soul tie with _____, and any resentment against You, God, for allowing this to happen in my life. I forgive _____ for their involvement in this sin. Jesus, wash me afresh in Your blood. I receive Your forgiveness, and I forgive myself for participating in this sin. Lord, I choose to cut the ungodly soul tie. I call back the layers of my soul that I gave away to _____. Lord, remove anything that has come into my soul through this soul tie. Thank you for restoring the layers of my soul in Jesus' name. Amen.

My daughters will now share a negative experience they had:

Not long after we met, we formed an ungodly soul tie with a spiritual mentor. Not fully knowing who we were in Christ (perfect, holy, and righteous), we belittled ourselves and exalted the mentor.

Holy Spirit gave us warnings about the mentor. We witnessed some ungodly fruit, but because of the soul tie, we couldn't discern the truth. We were being influenced in our mind. This opened the door to confusion and feelings of rejection with the potential of destroying our friendship.

While soaking in God's Presence, He revealed to us the open door to the enemy. So, we closed the door by saying the previous prayer. Thanks be to God!

Are you ready to be whole? Quiet yourself down and commune with Me. I am listening . . .

Love,

Your Daddy, who is your defender and protector,

God

Revelation 13:

Strongholds

We can demolish every deceptive fantasy that opposes
God and break through every arrogant attitude that
is raised up in defiance of the true knowledge of God.
We capture, like prisoners of war, every thought and
insist that it bow in obedience to the Anointed One.
—2 Corinthians 10:5 TPT

M y beloved children, I said, in the above verse, to capture every thought and insist that it bow in obedience
to Jesus, who is my Word. It is so important that you do this
if you want to have victory in your life. Even as a believer,
you will have to discern thoughts that pop into your mind.
You discern by asking yourself if the thought lines up with
My Word and My loving nature.

For example, if a thought pops into your mind such as, "God
loved you until you committed that sin, but now he doesn't
love you anymore," you must ask if it lines up with My nature
and My Word. No! My Word says, "I love you with an everlasting love." So cast this thought out. Immediately replace
it with the truth that I love you now and forever.

If you agree with the lie coming from the enemy, it can become a stronghold. Lies start as a root system that runs throughout your soul, sprouting up in all areas of your life. If the lies are believed as truth, a root system will bury deep, allowing a platform for Satan to work upon and a stronghold to be built.

2 Corinthians 10:4 AMP
The weapons of our warfare are not physical [weapons of flesh and blood]. Our weapons are divinely powerful for the destruction of fortresses.

Strongholds can become a fortress for the enemy to have power: thus, controlling your life and preventing you from fulfilling your destiny. Changing your beliefs to line up with the truth sets you free (see John 8:32). The truth tears down these strongholds.

To replace wrong beliefs, pray this:

1. I repent of my sin of believing the lie that _____ and for the resulting sins based upon the wrong belief.

2. I forgive anyone that contributed to me forming the wrong belief, and I forgive myself for my part in this lie.

3. I replace this wrong belief with the truth that _____ _____.

(This truth can come from My Words in the Bible and through soaking in My Presence for a more specific word. Caution: I will never tell you anything during your soaking time that contradicts My Words and My loving nature as Your Papa.)

Sometimes, when we believe a lie, we will make an inner vow. Refer to Shirley's testimony as an example in Revelation 9. I have said in My Word to not make an inner vow, because it affects your thinking and your actions negatively. I am not able to bring forth your full potential if being influenced by an inner vow.

To renounce an inner vow, pray this:

1. I acknowledge and repent of my sin of making a vow that
   _____.

2. I forgive _____ for playing a part in my forming this vow. I forgive myself for making this vow.

3. I now choose by the power of the Holy Spirit to _____ (the opposite of the vow).

Come to Me and ask Me for the truth concerning every-thing. I am waiting for you . . .

Your Loving Daddy, who is faithful and true,

God

Revelation 14:

Soul Cleansing

So give yourselves to God. Stand against the
devil, and he will run away from you. Come
near to God and he will come near to you. You
are sinners, so clean sin out of your lives.
—James 4:7–8 ERV

My beloved child, I want and need to tell you about your soul. You are a three part being: spirit, soul, and body. When you were saved by Jesus, your spirit became perfect, holy, and righteous forever, but your soul needs to be continually cleansed.

Romans 5:19 TPT
One man's disobedience opened the door for all
humanity to become sinners. So also one man's
obedience opened the door for many to be made
perfectly right with God and acceptable to him.

Hebrews 10:14 TPT
And by his one perfect sacrifice he made us
perfectly holy and complete for all time!

Your soul consists of your mind, will, and emotions. There are layers in your soul. Some of My children have more layers than others—that is why they are more emotional or passionate.

In the beginning, your soul is clean and perfect when Holy Spirit knits you to the dot of flesh in your mother's womb. Your soul is fed twenty-four hours a day. Everything you watch and hear is deposited in the layers of your soul, good or bad. These images and words affect your thoughts, emotions, and will.

There is a battle for the soul. For an example, hurtful words can form emotionally weak spots in your soul which become entry points for deception. The devil uses deception to lead you astray and into bondage. When negative emotions are not loosed from the soul, they become a soul wound.

A person receives wounds to their soul through their own sins, sins committed against them, and generational sins. Soul wounds give the enemy an open door to make you sick mentally and physically, a legal right to bring destruction in every area of your life.

Soul wounds can start as early as conception. An example is an unwanted child. The rejection that is felt by the unwanted baby in the womb makes a wound. Soul wounds occur at any age through traumatic events, offenses, unforgiveness, etc. We are taught that time heals all wounds, but it is not true. Soul wounds must be healed by the blood and glory light of Jesus.

Malachi 4:2 AMPC
But unto you who revere and worshipfully fear My name shall the Sun of Righteousness arise with healing in His

wings and His beams, and you shall go forth and gambol like calves [released] from the stall and leap for joy.

John 17:22–23 NKJV
And the glory which You gave Me I have given them, that they may be one just as We are one: I in them, and You in Me; that they may be made perfect in one, and that the world may know that You have sent Me, and have loved them as You have loved Me.

Romans 8:11 TPT
Yes, God raised Jesus to life! And since God's Spirit of Resurrection lives in you, he will also raise your dying body to life by the same Spirit that breathes life into you!

To heal the wounds created by sins, thus cleansing your soul, pray this prayer:

1. Lord, forgive me of all my sins. I forgive others that have sinned against me. Jesus, wash all my sins away with Your precious blood. I plead your blood over the sins in my family line all the way back to Adam in Jesus' name.

2. I command the glory light *(dunamis* resurrection power) of Jesus from my spirit to flood my soul and body now. The glory light of Jesus is healing my wounds now in Jesus' name. Amen.

Some of your wounds are deeper and have been there longer. Therefore, they may require more application of Jesus' blood and glory light than others. I recommend the application daily to keep your souls clean and free of wounds. You live in a world full of hurt people who hurt others. This is a lifestyle change.

Hebrews 3:12–14 TPT

So search your hearts every day, my brothers and sisters, and make sure that none of you has evil or unbelief hiding within you. For it will lead you astray, and make you unresponsive to the living God. This is the time to encourage each other to never be stubborn or hardened by sin's deceitfulness. For we are mingled with the Messiah, if we will continue unshaken in this confident assurance from the beginning until the end.

Once your soul is whole, your body can be in health as well. If you have any symptoms in your body, take your authority and command the symptoms or sickness to go in the name of Jesus.

Decrees/prayers for your body:

Thank You, Father, for a strong heart. I command you to beat perfectly. The life of God flows in my blood and cleanses my arteries of all matter that doesn't pertain to life in Jesus' name.

Every organ and tissue of my body functions in the perfection that God created it to function. I forbid all malfunction in my body in Jesus' name. I command every cell in my body to be normal, supporting life and health in Jesus' name. Any cancer leaves me now in Jesus' name.

Arthritis, be gone from me! I command all pain and swelling to leave me now in Jesus' name. All sickness and disease must leave my body in Jesus' name, for by Jesus' stripes I have been healed. I receive the *dunamis* resurrection power of Jesus into my body now.

Lungs, be healed and whole. All infection be gone in Jesus' name. I speak life and strength to my immune system.

The Lord heals me inside and out from every disease, kisses my heart with forgiveness in spite of all I've done, redeems my life from the pit, and renews my youth like the eagles (see Psalm 103:3–5).

3 John 1:2 NKJV
Beloved, I pray that you may prosper in all things
and be in health, just as your soul prospers.

Testimonies:

Thomas, a seer of the supernatural, gave this testimony after receiving revelation about soul wounds: Wanting to share with his father, Thomas observed dark spots in his father's soul. (The layers of a person's soul appear as layers of an onion.) He led his father through the soul–cleansing prayer and observed gray smoke leaving his father's body with the disappearing of some but not all the dark spots. Therefore, the prayer was repeated, and his soul (onion) became clean.

Shirley's testimony about how effective the cleansing prayer is for the restoration of families: Sally had been estranged from her daughter and grandchildren for over 6 years. Shirley prayed over this situation, pleading the blood of Jesus over the family and releasing the glory light of Jesus to each one's soul. The next day, Sally was ecstatic; she received the long-awaited call from her daughter for family restoration.

All My love,

Your Daddy, who prospers and heals you,

God

Revelation 15:

Breaking Word Curses

Whoever guards his mouth and tongue
keeps his soul from troubles.
—Proverbs 21:23 NKJV

Out of the same mouth come forth blessing and cursing.
These things, my brethren, ought not to be so.
—James 3:10 AMPC

My children make the mistake daily to speak words freely as though they don't have any meaning. Words have tremendous power: death and life are in the power of the tongue (see Proverbs 18:21). Every word you speak or hear goes into your soul, and it affects you positively or negatively.

It is vital to line up your words with My promises in My Word rather than with the negative circumstances around you. It is also imperative to loose negative words spoken over you. Words that are spoken can either bring restoration or cause damage; heal or break your heart; bring joy or sadness; enhance or destroy your dreams.

To break word curses, say this prayer aloud:

Father, I choose as an act of my will to loose all negative words spoken by me or over me in Jesus' name. I forgive and release everyone who has ever spoken negatively to me or about me, including _____ (others' names). I also forgive myself. Father, I choose to bind _____ (the opposite) to my soul in Jesus' name. I receive your divine blessings. Amen.

Example: If someone called you stupid, you can pray this:

Father, I choose as an act of my will to loose this negative experience from my soul in Jesus' name. I reject all negative words. I also forgive them as you have graciously forgiven me. Father, I choose to bind your thoughts, your truth, and your love to my soul right now in Jesus' name. Amen.

The same prayer will work to loose traumatic events and violence from your soul. Then you will bind My love, joy, peace, truth, and goodness to your soul in Jesus' name.

Proverbs 18:21 TPT
Your words are so powerful that they will kill or give life, and the talkative person will reap the consequences.

I invite you now to repeat My Words over you aloud: "God says that I am beautiful; God says I am dearly loved by Him; God says that I am stunning to Him; God says that I have greatness on the inside of me; God says that my future is glorious and amazing; God says that it is not too late to fulfill the wonderful destiny He has for me; I receive His Words now in Jesus' name."

Love,

Your Daddy, who created the world with My Words,

Almighty God

Revelation 16:

The Power of Decrees

Where the word of a king is, there is power; And
who may say to him, "What are you doing?"
—Ecclesiastes 8:4 NKJV

I have called My children to rule and reign as kings in life,
and kings make decrees. The words of kings are authoritative and powerful, and you are a royal priesthood. A king's
words have the power to move mountains, to build, to tear
down, to heal, and to restore. One of the most powerful
prayers is a prayer of decrees.

1 Peter 2:9 TPT
But you are God's chosen treasure—priests who are
kings, a spiritual "nation" set apart as God's devoted
ones. He called you out of darkness to experience
his marvelous light, and now he claims you as his
very own. He did this so that you would broadcast
his glorious wonders throughout the world.

When decrees are made, the words become weapons that the angels use to battle on your behalf. Demons flee when decrees are made: the enemy has no defense against them.

Decrees are powerful statements that break off bondages. You can change the outcome of a situation with a decree. They bring My blessings to you.

You can take My promises in the Bible and personalize them, decreeing them over yourself and your family. My scribe angels write your decrees down when you speak them, and they become your reality.

Example: I decree that I am God's beloved child, so that makes me royalty. I am *forever* young, beautiful, healthy, wealthy, and wise–this is who God created me to be and to walk in all the days of my life. Father, your will and your way be done in me today and every day. Amen

Love,

Your Daddy God, whose promises are Yes in Christ.

Revelation 17:

Healing

He heals their broken hearts and
bandages their wounds.
—Psalms 147:3 ERV

But He was wounded for our transgressions, He was
crushed for our wickedness [our sin, our injustice, our
wrongdoing]; The punishment [required] for our well-being
fell on Him, And by His stripes (wounds) we are healed.
—Isaiah 53:5 AMP

Bless and affectionately praise the LORD, O my
soul, And do not forget any of His benefits; Who
forgives all your sins, Who heals all your diseases;
Who redeems your life from the pit, Who crowns
you [lavishly] with lovingkindness and tender mercy;
Who satisfies your years with good things, So that
your youth is renewed like the [soaring] eagle.
—Psalm 103:2–5 AMP

My Son, Jesus, paid the price for your healing. It is
possible to live a life of health and longevity. Many

of My children believe that sickness is a form of punishment or to teach them a lesson, but My will is always for you to walk in divine health. Just as you want your children healthy and whole, how much more do I want this for you, My child.

Luke 6:19 NKJV
And the whole multitude sought to touch Him, for power went out from Him and healed them all.

Sickness is never from Me. It is from the enemy. Satan will attempt to deceive you into believing you have no choice but to accept the sickness or disease. But I say, "You have a choice." If you have accepted My Son, Jesus, as your Lord and Savior, then you have My perfect DNA without sickness and disease.

Exodus 15:26 NKJV
[. . .] I am the Lord who heals you.

Beloved, I wish above all things that you succeed and prosper and be in good health, just as your soul prospers (see 3 John 1:2). To take authority over sickness and disease, start with soul cleansing and break generational curses to get your soul whole. (Please revisit Revelation 11 and Revelation 14.) Sicknesses are leaving your body when these two prayers are said. For any remaining symptoms, come to Me, and I will reveal the root cause and the effective prayer in this book to decree against the enemy.

1 Corinthians 1:9 MSG
God [. . .] shares with us the life of his Son and our Master Jesus. He will never give up on you. Never forget that.

If I didn't withhold my best (Jesus) from you, I will *not* withhold healing from you! I am always willing to heal, bless, protect, and restore you and your family.

Romans 8:32 AMPC
He who did not withhold or spare [even] His own Son but gave Him up for us all, will He not also with Him freely and graciously give us all [other] things?

For healing, ask Jesus to come lay His hands on you. (You may actually feel His Presence.) Then say, "Jesus, I invite you to wash me and my family line afresh in your healing blood. I command your *dunamis* resurrection power in my spirit to flood my soul and body right now in Jesus' name. I command all sickness and disease to leave my body now in Jesus' name. (Be more specific concerning any symptoms and their root cause as Jesus leads you.)

All My love,

Your Daddy, who heals you,

God

Revelation 18:

Daily Prayer for Abundant Life

I n conclusion to all that you have learned about who I am, who you are, and how the enemy comes against you, I have included this simple prayer to be repeated daily to live out the abundant life that Jesus paid for:

Lord, forgive me of all my sins, and I forgive all others who have sinned against me. Father, I loose all anger, feelings of abandonment, loneliness, depression, unforgiveness, guilt, shame, condemnation, rejection, fear, doubt, unbelief, deception, lust, resentment, judgments, poverty mentality, religious teaching, confusion, rebellion, pride, jealousy, negative words, profanity, complaining, worries, sadness, disappointments, frustrations, heaviness, anxiety, and stress from my soul right now in Jesus' name. Jesus, wash me afresh in Your blood. I plead the blood of Jesus over me and all my family right now because of the mighty power in Your blood to protect, heal, restore, and bless us. Jesus, wash all the sins away in my blood line all the way back to Adam.

I command the glory light of Jesus (*dunamis* resurrection power) that is already in my spirit to go into my soul, to flood my soul now in Jesus' name. The glory light of Jesus floods my soul and my body, too. The glory light of Jesus is healing all the wounds of my whole life right now in Jesus' name. Father, I bind Your love, grace, mercy, health, abundance, faith, favor, blessings, goodness, joy, peace, glory, fun, discernment, plans, wisdom, energy, light, strength, prosperity, and life to my soul right now in Jesus' name.

The *dunamis* healing power of Jesus go into every organ and cell of my body and make me divinely healthy and whole now in Jesus' name. I decree that through Jesus' poverty, I became rich. Amen.

Life and death are in the power of your tongue. Therefore, choose life every day with the words coming out of your mouth. I made it easy!

Hugs and kisses,

Your loving Daddy, who gives you life abundantly

Revelation 19:

Journal Entries and
God Encounters in 2016

W̅e want to say that our happiness and our salvation does not depend on these angelic visitations and supernatural encounters. May these encounters never be held in higher esteem than the written Word of God: for Jesus and the Word are One. May all of us remain open to correction. We pray that every encounter leads you along the path of God's love and into the incomparable greatness of His kingdom, and that these encounters empower you to have your own!

John 14:21 AMPC
The person who has My commands and keeps them is the one who [really] loves Me; and whoever [really] loves Me will be loved by My Father, and I [too] will love him and will show (reveal, manifest) Myself to him. [I will let Myself be clearly seen by him and make Myself real to him.]

Galatians 1:6–10 ERV

A short time ago God chose you to follow him. He chose
you through his grace that came through Christ. But
now I am amazed that you are already turning away and
believing something different from the Good News we
told you. There is no other message that is the Good
News, but some people are confusing you. They want
to change the Good News about Christ. We told you the
true Good News message. So anyone who tells you a
different message should be condemned—even if it's one
of us or even an angel from heaven! I said this before.
Now I say it again: You have already accepted the Good
News. Anyone who tells you another way to be saved
should be condemned! Now do you think I am trying to
make people accept me? No, God is the one I am trying
to please. Am I trying to please people? If I wanted to
please people, I would not be a servant of Christ.

My dear children, I want you to experience Me. I desire to
manifest Myself to you. As you seek Me, I will show you great
and marvelous things in the spiritual realm, but I need to
caution you with this: The prince of this world is Satan. He
wants to sabotage our intimacy and the experiences I have
for you, so he may appear to you as an angel of light or even
Jesus. It is vital to test all spirits.

2 Corinthians 11:14 ERV

That does not surprise us, because even Satan
changes himself to look like an angel of light.

When a spiritual being appears to you, your first response
needs to be "are you sent by God who gave His Son, Jesus,
to die for the sins of the world?" If the spiritual being is not
from Me, it cannot answer with a yes. If the spiritual being

does not answer or says no, command it to leave and not return in Jesus' name.

1 John 4:1–3 ERV

My dear friends, many false prophets are in the world now. So don't believe every spirit, but test the spirits to see if they are from God. This is how you can recognize God's Spirit. One spirit says, "I believe that Jesus is the Messiah who came to earth and became a man." That Spirit is from God. Another spirit refuses to say this about Jesus. That spirit is not from God. This is the spirit of the enemy of Christ. You have heard that the enemy of Christ is coming, and now he is already in the world.

Let's pray: Father, I choose as an act of my will to loose all deception from my soul. Holy Spirit, I ask You to lead me into all truth and give me revelation and discernment. I say, "Father, Your will, Your way be done in me and in my family on earth as it is in heaven." I ask You for wisdom to apply Your truth in every area of my life in Jesus' mighty name. Amen.

Habakkuk 2:1–4 ERV

I will stand like a guard and watch. I will wait to see what the LORD will say to me. I will wait and learn how he answers my questions. The LORD answered me, "Write down what I show you. Write it clearly on a sign so that the message will be easy to read. This message is about a special time in the future. This message is about the end, and it will come true. Just be patient and wait for it. That time will come; it will not be late. This message cannot help those who refuse to listen to it, but those who are good will live because they believe it.

Deuteronomy 29:29 ERV
There are some things that the LORD our God has
kept secret. Only he knows these things. But he
told us about some things. And these teachings
are for us and our descendants forever . . .

October 14th Encounter for Shirley

I attended a Glory Conference, and the minister requested that anyone wanting an impartation to come to the front. The moment the minister placed her hands on me, I felt electric bolts go through me from head to toe. This electricity continued to flow through me every few minutes for at least two hours. Then, for the next two days, every time I said the word *glory*, the power of God (in the form of electricity) ran through me.

October 16th

Stephanie's First Vision of Heaven—See Revelation 9.

November 12th Encounter

While we were attending a conference at Morningstar Ministries, we heard about angelic visitations at Prayer Mountain in Moravian Falls. We decided to embark on this journey.

We arrived at the mountain and walked to the top. We stepped off the trail to ask God what to do next. While praying together with our eyes closed, Shirley received a vision of a purple dot in the center of a purple circle. We opened our eyes and discovered a tree to the right of us with a purple mark on it. We stepped over into the leaves in front of the tree. After doing this, we noticed there were other trees with purple markings, forming a circle.

Holding out our hands to God, we felt waves of God's glory on us. With Stephanie's eyes open, she had a vision of angels coming and going. With Shirley's eyes closed, she saw an orb of white light, swirling and turning to bluish color. Then Stephanie saw two huge angels appear on each side of us. We asked their names. The name "Eric" popped into Stephanie's mind, and the name "Patriot" came into Shirley's mind. (Since this was our first time to talk to angels, we both questioned if we had heard right. It was later confirmed by a prophetic seer.)

Shirley did not see the angels. When she asked where the angels were standing, she felt a firm hand touch her on her left side. Stephanie confirmed that an angel was standing on Shirley's left.

Next, Stephanie saw a big hand come down from heaven, holding a pitcher of oil. It was tipped and poured on us. (We didn't feel it, so we just received it by faith.) Then, a bouquet of flowers appeared to Stephanie. We both could smell a sweet fragrance. We reached our hands up, saying, "Thank you, Papa, for the flowers."

With Shirley's eyes closed, she then saw a turquoise blue peacock feather and an eagle eye, hearing in her mind, "You are receiving eagle-eye vision." This supernatural encounter ended with Father telling us, "This is the beginning of a great future. It is a new day for the both of you. Make sure that you come to Me for everything, not man. I am a great teacher. I am launching you forth."

As we were discussing what took place and trying to take it all in, we decided to look up the meaning of the angels' names. Eric means "eternal ruler." (Prior to this encounter, Stephanie had been told by Father that she would receive an "eternal" angel who would accompany her until she went to heaven.) The name Patriot means "someone who regards himself as a defender, especially of individual rights." What an amazing God we have!

Desiring a confirmation of this supernatural encounter, we asked a high-level seer who talks to Jesus and angels to tell us what he saw and heard about our encounter at Prayer Mountain. This seer was not given any information other than "we had an encounter on Prayer Mountain." The seer described the huge angels in detail just like Stephanie had seen, and confirmed their names to be "Patriot, who is assigned to Shirley, and Eric, who is assigned to Stephanie." All glory to God!

December 1st Encounter

Stephanie was playing the song "Here as in Heaven" while driving to work early that morning. As she sang the words to the song, she found herself in heaven standing with a crowd of people watching a concert. The same song was being played in heaven as in her car. All of heaven was singing and declaring over the earth. When the song finished, the encounter was over.

December 2nd Encounter

Stephanie and her family were on their way to dinner. Christmas songs were playing over the radio. She suddenly found herself in heaven dancing with Jesus.

December 4th Encounter

During Stephanie's soaking time with the Lord, she was taken to the throne room of heaven. God placed His hand on her head, and then said, "Write this down."

Father told her several things about her future. Then He concluded with this: Keep seeking Me. I have so much to share with you. It is just the beginning. Do not worry about a thing. Where you will get this or find that. I will take care of all that. I do not have many like you. The more you are available, the more you will do. Do not put me in a box. If you believe it, it will happen. I can do anything, and I will. All you have to do is believe. There is nothing that I can't do. Just believe. All I need is someone who will allow Me to work through them. A willing participant.

December 8th Encounter

Stephanie was decreeing and declaring God's promises. Suddenly, she found herself dancing with rainbow-colored ribbons in the throne room. The saints in heaven were running to get hit by the light leaving the ribbons. Once hit with the light, they were filled with the love of Jesus.

Revelation 20:

Some Journal Entries and God Encounters in 2017

But God chose those whom the world considers foolish
to shame those who think they are wise, and God chose
the puny and powerless to shame the high and mighty.
—1 Corinthians 1:27 TPT

But if he does not listen, take along with you one or
two others, so that every word may be confirmed and
upheld by the testimony of two or three witnesses.
—Matthew 18:16 AMPC

January 3rd

While soaking at home in God's Presence, Shirley asked the Holy Spirit to activate her spiritual senses so that she could know God better. With her eyes closed, she then saw a beautiful, peaceful place that must be in heaven due to the indescribable beauty. Next, she heard, "It's in the mail." (This statement was a confirmation from Papa to

Shirley regarding a prior prophetic word she had received on November 11, 2016)

January 20th

Early in the morning, Stephanie was spending time with the Lord and found herself walking the streets of heaven with Jesus. She noticed American flags flying from the businesses and shops in heaven. The atmosphere in heaven was full of excitement and anticipation of the inauguration of President Donald Trump. Everyone in heaven was preparing for the celebration. Jesus asked her to follow him as he took her to a large amphitheater made of ivory. Jesus explained to her that the center of the amphitheater was open for all of heaven to view the inauguration. The encounter ended, and Stephanie was back in her room.

February 12th

While soaking with the Lord, Shirley went into a trance. She saw a two-lane highway with a lot of cars traveling on it. Then the scene changed to a small log cabin with a front porch. The cabin was amid tall, green trees. (Not having any idea of where this cabin was or what God was telling her, Shirley would find herself at this cabin in Branson, Missouri, for the weekend starting July 28, 2017.)

February 13th

In a trance, Shirley saw skyscrapers and a huge stadium. The stadium was filled with orange and blue seats. The people were running to the front and on the stage with healing testimonies.

February 18th

While Shirley's husband, Mark, was soaking, he saw himself standing on a balcony. The balcony was small and curved in an oval shape. It had black wrought iron bars at the top. From the balcony, he could see the blue ocean water with boats to the right, and a tall wooden pier. (On a vacation in April 2017, Mark would be standing in a condo, seeing the same balcony, boats, and pier. He had never been there or seen a picture of this place before. The plans for this condo vacation were made in March.)

March 3rd

In a trance, Shirley saw a row of cars going up a hill on a two-lane highway through a beautiful valley. The scene changed to a cozy living room with a wooden floor and a big area rug. The sun was beaming through a big picture window into the living room area. (This is the inside of the cabin in Branson, Missouri, that she would visit in July.)

March 6th

In a trance, Shirley saw a bathroom sink first. Then, there was an antique chandelier over a kitchen table. (This is another picture of the inside of the cabin in Branson, Missouri.) Shirley heard, "I'm cleansing your hearts."

March 25th

During Shirley's soaking time with Papa, she heard, "Enjoy the ride. Stop and smell the roses along the way of your journey. Enjoy My Presence along the path." Then at the end of the soaking time, Shirley saw a glimpse of a rustic dining table with a chandelier over it. (The inside of the cabin at

Branson again. Shirley is still unaware that she will soon visit this cabin.)

April 19ᵗʰ

Shirley sat down in her comfortable living room chair, and asked, "What do You want to say to me today, Papa?" Papa replied, in His sweet loving voice, "My dear daughter, I want you to know how precious you are to Me. There is no one exactly like you. I made you unique. That is why you are so special to Me. My beloved daughter, these words are healing your heart right now. So, meditate on My words. I want you whole, victorious, dynamic, and spectacular, because I have made you to be that. Do you see it, My daughter? Listen to My words, and you will be exactly that. Because you already are."

Next, Shirley asked Lord Jesus to speak to me. This is what she heard. "Shirley, My bride, you are altogether lovely to Me. I love you forever and always will love you. Come dance with Me, My lovely bride. I want you to feel special, to feel safe, to feel accepted, and to feel unconditionally loved by Me." . . . Then, she asked Holy Spirit to speak to her. This was His reply: "Dear Shirley, first off: I love you passionately. You are one with Me. I have been leading you for a while now and will continue. It is My joy to lead you because you are so special to Me. I love your passion. Allow Me to work through you (for I am in you), and others will see Me. You are righteous—completely and perfectly righteous. Remember how righteous I have made you in Christ, and you will do great things—the greater works. I am God working in you, giving you the desire and the performance, the will and the to do for My great pleasure. You are a joy to My heart, dear daughter. I am so pleased with you."

April 20th

Shirley woke up thinking about a book titled *And God Said, "It is Easy."* (Shirley has never had the desire to write a book.) Shirley asked, "What are You saying, Lord? Do you want me to write a book? Maybe with Stephanie? If so, will You tell her? I am not going to say a word to her about this. That way I will know for sure that this is really You. Especially since I have never thought about writing a book, I need a confirmation from You."

May 4th

During Stephanie's morning soaking time with Father, she heard, "Hasn't it been fun finding my clues of the future? If you think this is fun, just you wait. I have much more to come. It will blow your socks off! This is a great time to be alive. The power you will witness will amaze and astonish you. Just go with the flow. Enjoy the ride. You will have many stories to tell. Some will be hard for the human mind to believe. But believe it! It is coming."

God's Plan for Us to Write a Book Comes Alive

In the afternoon, Stephanie read to her husband, James, a few of the journal entries from soaking times with the Lord (something she had never done before). James replied, "You are going to write a book. There are people who need to hear these words from God." Stephanie answered, "Shut your mouth. Me, write a book? Not me!"

Later that evening, Stephanie called Shirley to share about the conversation with her husband, laughing about the possibility of writing a book. Shirley replied, "Well, actually it is true. I want to read you the journal entry from God about two weeks ago. This is confirmation! Wow!"

May 5th

Stephanie got alone with God, in her quiet place, and asked Him about the subject of writing a book. He answered, "Don't be scared. It is easy! It is just what you have been doing. Simply write the words I say. Sit down at the computer, and type what I tell you."

May 23rd

Stephanie and her family went to dinner. Her son, Andrew, had hurt his leg playing sports. Stephanie prayed over him, commanding the pain to leave in Jesus' name. She felt heat in her hands as she prayed. The pain left instantly!

May 27th

As Stephanie and a high-level seer were riding through town, she was speaking decrees over her hands, saying, "These hands are powerful weapons. They will heal the sick; they will raise the dead. These hands will cast out demons." As the declarations were being made, the seer saw a beam from heaven hit Stephanie's hands.

Then, Stephanie began to pray for a pedestrian walking down the sidewalk. The seer saw glowing glory balls about the size of a small basketball come out of her hands and enter the pedestrian. This excited Stephanie, so she started having fun sending glory balls into everyone she encountered. They were told by Jesus that it was not necessary to be specific about the needs of the person because when the glory balls are sent, all needs of the person will be met.

May 31ˢᵗ

In her quiet time with the Lord, Shirley saw lots of colors. She asked, "What are all these colors that I am seeing?" The Lord responded, "It is My glory. What I have for you and Stephanie you can't comprehend right now. But in due time, the appointed time, you will see it. Rest in My words to you. Review them often. They are life to your destiny. Don't let yourself get discouraged in the so called 'waiting.' Mighty things are happening right now in the spirit realm. So, hang on! Hang onto My words to the two of you. They are mighty to the pulling down of strongholds. I am for you. Keep on believing! It is happening! You will see, and all the world will see. You see? Lol!"

June 11ᵗʰ

Waiting on a flight at the Tampa airport with a connecting flight in Houston onto Nashville, Tennessee, Stephanie was typing on her laptop. Out of the blue, she had a thought that her flight in Houston would be delayed, and she would have to spend the night in the Houston airport. She thought to herself, "That was odd." Blowing this off, she continued working.

She then had a vision of herself stranded in the Houston airport. The vision ended as she heard her name called over the intercom to come to the Southwest Airlines counter. The agent stated that the Houston flight had been delayed. He explained that if she got on the flight to Houston, she would miss her connecting flight to Nashville. This would leave her in Houston until tomorrow. He informed her of a direct flight from Tampa to Nashville. Her flight was changed, and she arrived in Nashville as planned. The crisis was averted. God is so good!

June 13th

In her quiet time with Jesus, Shirley saw (with her eyes closed) Wonder Woman's hand with gold rings on her fingers. Then, an image that turned into a crown, some purple clouds, and a bright sunny valley. The vision ended with thousands of people packed in an outdoor area with Jesus in the center.

June 25th

While Stephanie was driving the long ride home from Georgia, Father God began talking to her, so she grabbed her phone and recorded the flowing thoughts: "My sweet, precious child, isn't this exciting? A book. I know you can't imagine writing a book, but this is what I need you to do. Write a book. This is only the beginning. I've got much more in store, but it will begin with the book. Continue to spend time with Me. Listen to what I say to you. It excites Me to reveal a piece of the plan to you. My plan is full of excitement and joy and wonder. Wonder that you cannot even imagine but that will amaze you. Continue to spend time with Me. That's all you have to do. Listen to My voice. Remember it is easy! That's the message—it is easy. That's what My children need to hear. They need to hear that My love is easy. That I am easy. I desire for My children to know Me for who I really am, not who I've been portrayed to be. I am the GREAT I AM who loves them unconditionally no matter what they've done! They still cannot see it. That's the point of the book. I need My children to see that I really love and want them. That I desire them and have plans for their future. Plans that are perfect, beautiful, and wonderful. Plans that will never fail. That's where the two of you come in. So, spend time with Me. Listen to My voice and do as I tell you. I will do the rest. I will guide you on what to say in the book. Just come together, and My words will flow. The unity of the three of us is very important. Remember this is a team!"

July 16th

Shirley asked, "Papa, what do you want to say to me today?" Papa responded, "My dear Shirley, the river you saw in the vision is you. You are the river. My life—My living water—flows out of you. Remember I told you that I want you to rest in the place of My love for you every day? Keep doing what you are already doing. Remind yourself of My love—My unchanging, unconditional love for you. You will go far. Nothing can stop you when you are grounded and established in My love and amazing grace toward you, dear one. I love you now and forever."

July 29th

Stephanie and Shirley, at the cabin on Prayer Mountain in Branson, had pen and paper ready to start writing the book. A seer, also present, saw angels begin lining up in and outside of the cabin to witness the start of the book. Then, they all heard "pop, pop, pop" coming from upstairs. The seer said that the angels were letting off poppers, holding banners, dancing, and celebrating. The cloud of witnesses were looking down through the portal from heaven. Stephanie and Shirley were amazed and surprised by all these things happening in the spiritual realm.

August 29th

Shirley's soaking time: "Dear beloved, I wish above all things that you prosper and be in health according to your soul prospering. So yes, what you are doing in the women's group regarding soul cleansing and inner healing is of Me. It is very powerful and effective in getting you and others that I put in your path walking in prosperity and divine health. So keep up the good work! I am flowing through you to get healing to My children. I thank you for being in Christ, for allowing Me to flow through you in such an awesome way—My divine way."

September 5th

Shirley asked Holy Spirit to speak to her during her quiet time and heard this: "My dear Shirley, I want you to do the inner healing of soul wounds for yourself, for the rejection and hurt you are feeling. And yes, fear. You have had a fear of seeing the bad and the ugly. There is no guilt here, My precious child, to be had, but I do want you to deal with this. For I have great plans for you. You need to be whole in your soul. I want you whole. Prosperity is coming to you in every area of your life. Remember I love you."

September 14th

Shirley's soaking time: "You are ready, My daughter. What I have planned for you will amaze you! You can get excited now, dear one! You won't be disappointed. No more delays! Proper alignment is key. The wait has been necessary. You are ready, My darling. Precious are you in My eyes. There have been setbacks, but you have been set up, My daughter, for a step up into your destiny. I'm so proud of you, dear one. The wait has been long for you, especially for how I created you. But you will see it has been worth the wait. Don't you see how you have just fell into the beginning stages of your destiny? Don't let anyone distract you.

September 19th

Shirley went to Anne's home to share inner healing prayers with her and two others for soul wounds, generational curses, and any unforgiveness. After they repeated the prayers together, Shirley prayed for healing for Bob's knee, commanding all knee pain and swelling to leave in Jesus' name. Anne, diagnosed with frozen shoulder, had not been able to lift her arm without pain for the last two years. Shirley released the *dunamis* power (glory light) of Jesus into Anne's shoulder for healing. Bob and Anne were instantly healed! All Glory to God! (Both remain healed to this day.)

September 28th

While Shirley was soaking at the Healing Hearts Group, Papa said this to the ladies that were present: "I want to say that I'm very pleased with this group. You are coming together in unity and in My love. You all are My kingdom warriors. Don't get stressed, striving to fulfill your destinies. I cannot say it enough that I am so pleased with the six of you, My beloved daughters. How precious you are in My eyes—My Wonder Women on the front lines. Keep coming to Me, and I will give you strategies, the blueprints to complete your destinies. By the way, your destinies are awesome! It will blow your minds if I let you know all of it now. That is why I give it to you in little nuggets. You will just fall into it if you let Me be your God and your Lord. No striving and no legalism are the keys. It truly is all by My grace. Remember how much I love you, and you will go far this year. Mary, rest in My love for you. I love you so much. You haven't really known My love for you like I have wanted you to because of the enemy's attacks on you throughout your life, but soak in My Presence, and you will experience it. This is a word for all of you. For My love never fails. I will never fail you because I love you no matter what forever and always. My love is extravagant for each one of you and everlasting. There is no love like My love. That is why it is so hard for you to understand it. But focus on My love. Whatever you focus on magnifies in your mind, your heart, and your soul."

October 5th

Shirley was told this at the Healing Hearts Group (Papa's Words to the group): "My gifts I have placed in each of you are irrevocable. Come away with Me, and I will reveal them to each one of you. It will surprise you—the wonderful gifts inside of you. I so much want to reveal them to you. I have longed to reveal them to you. You are ready. No more delays! It is time. My time for revelation to each one of you. Get ready for more surprises. Expect them. For they are coming. Supernatural signs and wonders. Confirmations of My extravagant love for you. It is kingdom time! My time on earth has come!"

November 13th

While Shirley was soaking with the Lord, she saw colors passing by her as she was soaring in the heavens. Then, she saw Christmas Town in heaven, looking down from above it. The scene changed, and Shirley was standing in the middle of a street in Christmas Town, looking up at an arched neon sign stretching from one side of the street to the other with words scrolling across it. Christmas Town was beautiful, full of brightly colored lights everywhere.

November 21st

During Shirley's soaking time, Papa said, "Do you remember the treasure chest you saw a couple years ago in a vision? I am pouring it out on you today—the gifts and the treasures from heaven." So, Shirley reached up by faith and said, "I receive the treasures from you, Papa, and I will give them out to others. Thank you, Papa! Wow!"

Later that evening, Shirley attended church, and Apostle Marvin preached on God's people having "this treasure in earthen vessels so that the excellence of the power may be of God and not of us." Then, the apostle asked if anyone had a word from the Lord to share with the group. Shirley, remembering Papa's words spoken earlier about the treasure chest, walked to the front and shared them. Upon hearing Papa's words, Apostle Marvin stepped over in front of Shirley, saying, "Let me be the first. Pray for me." Shirley laid her hands on his shoulders and quietly began releasing the glory of Jesus from her spirit. She moved her hands very softly to each side of his face, feeling electricity flowing through her body. Her hands began shaking, vibrating with the power of God. The apostle then called for everyone in the home church (about eighteen people) to come up and be prayed for under this glory of God. Some were laid out on the floor under this glory. A lady (who had been praying to receive visions from God for years) saw, in a vision, a huge treasure chest filled with gemstones and gifts being poured out over the city.

December 4th

Stephanie asked Father to show her what she agreed upon before coming to earth. She went into a vision. It was like a movie playing out in her mind. She saw herself as a little girl around five years old standing with the Father in front of a timeline. He sweetly explained the eras of time to her. He then asked her to choose when she wanted to be born. She chose the time frame where she was most needed by the Father. She noticed a little girl on the other side of the timeline tape. The little girl came under the tape and grabbed Stephanie's hand, telling Father that she wanted to come to the earth at the same time as Stephanie. That little girl was Shirley.

December 10th

In Shirley's soaking time, she saw a huge stadium full of people standing up and waving banners. These people were feeling the heavy Presence of God.

December 13th

While Stephanie was in her quiet place with Father, she heard, "My child, it pleases Me to see your passion for Me and the plans I have for My people. My people are hurting and need a touch from Me. One touch is all it will take. That's where you all come in. I want to use you to touch My people. Will you do that for Me? The rewards will be great. The rewards are greater than the task. It is so easy! Just listen to Me and do as I ask. I will direct your path. I will not mislead you. We are the dream team! Together we will make dreams come true. I want My people to see their worth, and I desire to lavish My blessings on them. My people are not ready to receive the blessings. Will you help Me?"

December 15th

Flowing thoughts to Stephanie: "I am revealing to you the ways of heaven. When I reveal the keys to success, continue to use them. Not everyone gets the keys. Only the ones who want them. I have so much to share with you. It is impossible to get it all in this lifetime. Many things will be revealed in heaven once we are all together. I am proud of you. It pleases Me to see how willing you are to help Me usher in this new time. Keep dreaming big! There is nothing we can't do together!"

Shirley's morning soaking time: Shirley saw a ladder in a vision, then heard this: "The more revelations you receive from Me, the higher you go into heavenly dimensions, especially the revelation of My love. Because My love takes you higher and higher. Oh, how I love My children. But they have not known, really known My love. I want your families to grow leaps and bounds in My love. That is My desire for your families and for you. For My love never fails!"

Shirley's evening soaking time: "I love you hearing My voice, listening to Me. I don't have that many. Thank you for your heart to sit down and listen to Me. It is sweet. It is music to My ears when I hear you coming to Me. Radical changes are coming! Precious times are coming. Sit at My feet, for the rewards are great. Better than that, sit on My lap, My dear child. Oh, how I love you! I don't need to kid-proof My home for you. Lol! I want you to have all the fun you want. Your mansions are not kid-proof. They are made for kids, My kids, to lose themselves in all the adventures and fun!"

December 16th

Daddy God's words to Stephanie: "Fun, fun, fun! That's what this is for Me. I am having so much fun with you. You are open to anything and everything I need you to do. I don't find that often. Most of My children make excuses and put Me in a box. But not you! That's one of the things I love about you. Because you are so open to Me and My ways, you will go far. You allow Me to do anything I need and want with no questions asked. Because you are so agreeable and make yourself available, I am able to bless you in ways never seen before. Keep pressing in and keep your eyes on Me at all times. Through this, we will crush the enemy. All of heaven is watching and cheering you on. Keep up the great work! Love, your Daddy."

While Shirley's friend, Allen, was soaking, he asked to fly on an angel's back. God told him, "You don't need angels to fly." He started flying through the sky, seeing the earth below. He saw water, boats, an old wrecked firetruck, and people standing around the firetruck in a cornfield.

December 18th

Stephanie's soaking time with Father: "My child, you are so sweet, and I love you so much. You are never alone. I am always with you. I am glad that you and Shirley have decided to focus on writing the book. This book is going to make a way for many that do not have a way. Like a beacon in the night."

Revelation 21:

Some Journal Entries and God Encounters in 2018

So don't remember what happened in earlier times. Don't think about what happened a long time ago, because I am doing something new! Now you will grow like a new plant. Surely you know this is true. I will even make a road in the desert, and rivers will flow through that dry land.
—Isaiah 43:18–19 ERV

For God shows no partiality [no arbitrary favoritism; with Him one person is not more important than another].
—Romans 2:11 AMP

January 1st

F ather's words to Stephanie: "I want to show and give you the world. The sky is the limit with the plans and future I have for you. You can go as high as you want. No limitations. Just ask and you shall receive. I want and choose to bless you. This is a great time to be alive. I can't wait to show you the things of heaven. Do you want to see them?"

January 2nd

Flowing thoughts to Stephanie: "This pleases Me so much. I love talking to My children. I am glad that you are teaching this to your family. I want to have an intimate relationship with them, a relationship where they can tell and ask Me anything. I want to direct their path. Continue to commune with Me, and I will show them My plans for their future: a future full of promise.

While Shirley's friend, Allen, was soaking with the Lord, he had a vision in which he saw himself sitting beside the Lion of Judah. Allen put his hand on the lion's hair and stroked it as the lion placed his head in Allen's lap.

January 3rd

Shirley's soaking time: "I am especially fond of you! Especially fond. Oh, how exciting this is! Celebrate with us because we are celebrating! It's party time! Party time, I tell you! There is no love like My love for My children. I love to love you. You let Me love you. You let Me be Me, who is Love Himself. There is a whole lot of love going on!" (Shirley felt like electricity was flowing through her body.)

January 4th

During Shirley's soaking time with God, she asked, "What do you want to tell me about the new year?" She heard, "I have great things, glorious things ahead for My children. The time is now. All the declarations you have made and believed are coming to pass in your life and in your family. No more delays in this kingdom age. I'm so excited to bless you with abundant life. Keep coming to Me. Confirmations are going to increase for you. Manifestations of My glory and miracles are on the horizon for you and your family. I'm so pleased with your faith, and it is going to a whole new level as the confirmations and manifestations show up. Your rewards are great, for you do seek Me. The revelations are coming to you on how simple and easy it is to know Me and My love. I love you, My beloved daughter. I am especially fond of you. Love, your Papa."

January 5th

Stephanie's soaking time: "I am so proud of you. I have not left you and neither will I ever leave you. You are the apple of My eye, and I am crazy about you. This is a time of training. You will make mistakes. Just learn from them and move on. Do not let them become part of you. I will not mislead you. I will continue to send confirmations to help you. When you get confirmations, you will know it is from Me. You've got this. Don't quit or give up. This is the best time to be alive, and I don't intend for you to miss it."

January 11th

God's Word to Stephanie: "I cherish the times I have with you. I desire to have a relationship with all My children. There will be a time when My children are home (in heaven), and everything is perfect. I long for a relationship with each and every one of My children. I desire to bless and lavish gifts on them, to heal them and do the things that good fathers do for their children."

January 13th

Shirley's son was sitting on a footstool in the living room and listening to his mom. As Shirley said, "Son, you and your family need to go to church with us tomorrow," he felt a firm hand poking him in the back. It startled him, and he turned around to see who was poking him. There were four witnesses to testify that no one was behind him in the natural. A seer stated that the angel's name was Cameron. Cameron is an angel residing at Shirley's home.

January 16th

On the way out the door, Shirley grabbed a brown scarf, still in a clear package, took it out, and placed it around her neck. Shirley met her friend, Anne, in town. Anne commented that she liked the scarf, so Shirley placed it around Anne's neck. Anne said that she felt chills go up and down her body. Then, she began swaying back and forth, feeling lightheaded. She experienced the chills (presence of God) during the whole time we were talking about Jesus.

January 22nd

Stephanie's soaking time: "I like to have fun. I want you to have fun. We always have fun in heaven. When you have fun, it shows and draws others near. You can share My love with others when they draw near. I want to use all My children to expand My kingdom in this time. Be available and open to what I ask, and you will touch many. Many of My children are lost and need to be found. Can you help Me find them?"

January 23rd

Shirley's friend, Anne, said, "I have been wearing the brown scarf you gave me every day for the last week. I feel God's Presence every time I wear it."

Stephanie's soaking time: It's an exciting time to be alive. These are exciting times for you and for Me. I love to see your reaction when I reveal My power. It makes Me happy to share with you, bless you, and pamper you. This is only the beginning. I am going to blow your mind with all I have for you.

January 31st

Shirley's soaking time: She had a vision of a chariot of salvation soaring through the night sky, then it came down to earth. Even the intricate wheels were seen in detail.

February 4th

Stephanie's soaking time: "Grace will cover everything. There is nothing it won't cover. My children do not understand this, so they live with the guilt of their past and wounds that kill. I desire to heal the wounds. With My healing, they will become whole. Wholeness is easy to receive. Just let Me move in, and I will drive out any darkness. I need you to share this message with the world. This will break the bondage. My children have been in bondage for far too long. Include this message in the book. I am so proud of how the book is coming. It is full of truths that set people free."

February 5th

Stephanie received a prophetic word that she was dancing on a hardwood floor, shattering the enemy, and kicking up dust. So the next morning, Stephanie and Shirley started marching and dancing around the coffee table, playing praise songs while making declarations for their families and others. They loosed all negativity from their souls, and invited Jesus to come in with His glory light. They felt God's loving presence. Stephanie had a tingling sensation in both her hands.

That evening, there were six of us soaking in God's Presence in the living room. Specks of gold and ruby dust started appearing on the living room rug and coffee table. Then we all heard a loud "ding" come from the kitchen area, as if someone had rung a dinner bell. Yet there was no one else in the house. Next, we all heard popping sounds from the kitchen area. Stephanie sat down on the sofa, and her arms and hands felt very heavy with intense shock waves going through them with the frequency changes of the worship music. After the three friends left, the gold and ruby dust continued to increase on and around the coffee table. Stephanie picked up a speck of ruby dust with her finger, and it multiplied to four before their eyes. Overnight, to their surprise, all the gold and ruby dust disappeared!

February 6th

While we were soaking together this evening, emerald, gold, and ruby dust appeared on and around the coffee table again. We also smelled a sweet fragrance in the room. Then, this is what Stephanie heard: "I love you. I love you. I love you. I have been watching you from My throne intently. I can't take My eyes off you. I cannot resist the attraction. The dance and declarations the two of you are doing are powerful. They will break all yokes. This is a move of My power that will continue to grow daily. The gold and ruby dust is real, and more manifestations are on the way. I have started a great work in you that will be fantastic when finished. You are so sweet to Me. You melt My heart. I want to bless you abundantly. All the experiences and encounters with Me should be in the book. My children need to hear them. You are My end-time warriors, and with a battle cry, you will destroy the enemy. Keep on dancing!"

February 9th

Stephanie's soaking time: "I love you so much. I can't wait to reveal more to you. The sky is the limit. You can do all things through Jesus. I do mean all things. This is a time of miracles and wonder, a time where I get to show My power! I want to use you and Shirley to reveal My power. This is a great time to be alive. I have assigned a special angel to go with you as you travel. His name is Journey. He will prepare your way. He will leave with you today. He is excited about his assignment. He knows the future I have for the team. Make arrangements to work on the book. This is most important at this time. Declare and decree the things of God over you and your family. I will honor them. Put Me to the test. The plans I have for you and your family are amazing. I want to build your faith so you can share My greatness with others. This will build their faith. I am getting ready to pour out My Spirit on this world. You are My end-time warriors. Keep spending time with Me. Your gifts will continue to grow. I love you!"

Assignment of an Angel

As Stephanie was leaving for the airport, an angel feather floated down from the ceiling and landed on her luggage. This was from the angel previously mentioned. A high-level seer also confirmed the angel assignment, saying the angel's name was Journey, and the angel liked the band Journey, too!

March 1st

God's message to His children: "The time is now! I am making a way for all My children. A way full of blessings and promise. Do you want it? It is your choice. I will not make the choice for you. Only you can decide. I have great plans for you. Do you accept the future I have for you? I promise blessings and adventure. It will never be boring. I love you and have nothing but the best in store for you. Will you choose Me and the dynamic future ahead?"

March 2nd

In prayer, Shirley was releasing the fireballs of God to her family. Shirley's husband, Mark, began seeing a slideshow on the living room wall. (Prior to this, Mark had never seen the spiritual realm in the form of a slideshow.) He saw Jesus first. Then, he saw his mom in heaven; Shirley's mom, Betty; Shirley's sister, Darla, wearing a crown on her head; his brother, Ronnie; and Shirley's brother, Donald. All the aforementioned family members are living in heaven. Penny, Mark's miniature schnauzer that died several years ago, was sitting in Ronnie's lap, licking his face. The last slide was Jesus, tilting his head back and blowing a white glory cloud over them. Wow! This slideshow of heaven lasted about thirty minutes!

March 3rd

Stephanie's soaking time: "Write, write, write! The words will come. I determine what to say and I am in every word written. Supernatural miracles and encounters will come to whoever allows the practices from the book to enter their soul and change the way they think! I bless this book and whoever reads it!"

March 10th

In the afternoon, Shirley was talking about a prophetic word she had read on Facebook earlier that day. It was about a ship that was filled to the brim. Then suddenly, Shirley saw her first open vision; it was a boat that appeared on the living room wall.

In the evening, Stephanie and Shirley were soaking together with two other seers. They put on praise music and began marching around the coffee table. They were singing with the music as well as making declarations for their families and others. Both seers saw a glory cloud over them. They invited Papa, Jesus, Holy Spirit, the Lion of Judah, angels, and the cloud of witnesses to join them. The seers saw Papa God, Jesus, angels, and the Lion of Judah come into the living room and walk around the table with them. They were happy and dancing to the music! Wow! After a few minutes, Shirley and Stephanie sat down and closed their eyes. Stephanie heard this: "This is the time for creative miracles. You have come a long way and have made the journey. You are ready. Begin to speak it, and it will happen. I will work miracles through this team. Remember to give Me the glory. Do not let pride creep in. The enemy will try to take your eyes off Me and onto yourself. Many have fallen because of pride. I have prepared you for such a time as this. We can do this together!"

Shirley heard this from Papa: "I yearn to bless you. Don't give up! It is going to happen! We love to see your excitement. Keep on decreeing! The bowls of heaven are tipping! Isaiah 43. Rest . . . Enjoy the adventure! We are enjoying watching the four of you."

March 11th

Stephanie's morning soaking time with Father, sitting on his lap as a little girl: "I love to bless you like a parent blesses his child. Do not stop seeking Me and declaring over your life. Your words make it all the way to the throne room. The fragrance coming from your decrees is sweet. I was there when you all marched around the table. Decree things over your family. This is very powerful! We rejoice and have so much fun watching. It's like a party. Continue what I have placed in you to do."

In the evening, Stephanie and Shirley began marching around the living room table, making decrees. Mark and the other seer were with them as well, watching for any supernatural activity. One seer saw clearly with his eyes open. Mark, with eyes closed, relaxed in the recliner to see in the spiritual realm. Gold dust started appearing on the rug and the table. This was followed by ruby and emerald dust. Even a tiny diamond was discovered lying on the rug in front of the sofa. Some of the gold, ruby, and emerald specks were picked up and placed on a piece of clear tape for safe keeping.

After a few minutes, Mark saw a huge bright portal open in front of them. An angel named Commander, on a large white horse, came in the room. Behind the horse, whose name was Pegasus, was the most vivid, beautiful valley Mark had ever seen with tall, green trees; bright, colorful flowers; and the greenest grass.

Pegasus had a rainbow-colored tail and mane. They were made aware that Pegasus was a warrior horse who fought on the front lines. The beautiful horse's armor had been removed before coming down through the portal into the living room. They were told by Commander that Jesus was coming.

Within moments, Jesus appeared in the living room, wearing a suit. Stephanie and Shirley were still marching, dancing, and making decrees. Papa God was invited to come, and He appeared, wearing formal attire. Jesus and Papa joined in with the dancing.

They all felt God's Presence, a heaviness in the atmosphere, and waves of electricity. Jesus took out a gift—the activation of the spiritual sense of taste—imparting it to everyone. Then, Papa took a gift out of a chest—the activation of the spiritual sense of feeling—to give to everyone.

At one point, the gold, ruby, and emerald dust stopped falling in the spirit realm. So, they asked for more. Then it started falling again.

A few minutes later, the Lion of Judah appeared in the heavenly portal, looking down at them. So, they asked Him to join them. He did! He was huge! They were in awe! By faith (since Shirley and Stephanie couldn't see Him), the two girls rode on the Lion's back around the table. The two seers watched this all take place in the spirit realm.

This was a lot to comprehend for Stephanie, Shirley, and Mark! The fourth witness interacts with the spiritual realm often. What an amazing and fun, yet profound time! This certainly was exceedingly abundantly above all that they could ever ask or imagine!

March 13th

Shirley's soaking time (I imagined myself sitting in Papa's lap because Ephesians 2:6 (TPT) says that I am raised up with Christ the exalted One, and I "ascended with him into the glorious perfection and authority of the heavenly realm, for we are now co-seated as one with Christ!"): "I am so pleased that you all have come together. We love it. Keep the momentum going. You saw how fast we showed up. Great blessings are coming to you all. You are positioning your-selves for them, and they are coming to you! The treasure chest of heaven has been opened. It is full of great things including strategies, and blueprints for the angels to bring to pass in your lives. My little children, you are blessing Me so much to get to spend time, precious time, with you."

The seer's soaking time with Papa: Immediately, he was in heaven, riding on a blue horse with a yellow mane. The horse's name was Richard. Papa was on Pegasus. They rode to his grandmother's diner in heaven and ate chili. Jesus' wall of "Jesus drinks" appeared, and they drank one. Then, they jumped in a bubble, went under the water, and saw mansions of the saints. The heavenly trip concluded with a ride on the back of an eagle.

March 18th

Shirley went into a trance-like state before getting out of bed and saw a chariot sitting on a paved road in front of a beau-tiful mansion. It was being pulled by a team of beautifully decorated, magnificent horses.

Stephanie's soaking time: "I love you with an everlasting love. You are special to Me—the apple of My eye. Keep seeking Me. Don't doubt the abilities I have equipped you with."

March 28th

Shirley's soaking time, in Papa's lap: "My precious daughter, you are so dear to Me. Keep it up—all these revelations, and you will soar in My glory, having all power over the enemy. No demons shall harm you. You will stomp on their heads and burn them up! I want freedom from all demonic oppression for My children. Keep applying Jesus' blood and releasing My glory light—for it truly is My resurrection power. There is no demonic power that can stay or stand around you when you do this. I already have the victory and have put the victory in you. So release it!"

March 29th

In her soaking time, Shirley asked, "Lord, how would you have me release Your love to myself and others?" This is what she heard: "My dear child, I love you. I want you to meditate on My love for you, to experience My love for you in tangible ways. The more you do, the more you will give out of My love in you. Remember that My Son Jesus made you righteous—all your sins are already forgiven—and come to Me with boldness, knowing this truth, resting in this truth. Receive my love for you daily, and then you will have it to give out to others. I want to baptize you afresh each day with the fire of My love. So receive it now, My dearly loved, precious daughter! You are Mine forever. And I am yours."

March 30th

Shirley's soaking time: Shirley had a vision of swirling colors, and she heard the word *passcode.* Not knowing what this meant, she continued talking to God about the negative words a minister had said about another. Shirley, being confused and sad about this situation, then heard Papa say, "My beloved daughter, do not trust in man, whether they are a minister or not. Keep on coming to Me first, and I will confirm the truth."

March 31st

Shirley's soaking time: Shirley asked about the word *passcode* from yesterday. She heard that the passcode was "Come to

Jesus daily." To this, Shirley replied, "I ask You—Papa, Jesus, and Holy Spirit—to go with me throughout the day, speaking to me, and highlighting things to me." Upon this reply, Shirley felt the glory of God flow through her whole body. Wow!

April 4th

Shirley's soaking time, sitting in Papa's lap: "My dear child, don't worry. I have everything taken care of, and I will take care of you. No worries! Come to Me when you are feeling down, and I will give you My love that heals you and gives you hope again. You and Mark can rest in My love. Don't give up, dear ones! You are Mine, and I am your loving Papa. So give all your cares and worries to Me. Love, your Papa."

April 5th

Shirley dreamed last night: Love is greater than being right. Life is all about the love of God. Her prayer: "Lord, let me be consumed with your love, and give it out to all I meet in Jesus' name. Amen."

April 6th

Stephanie's morning soaking time, sitting in Daddy's lap: "Tell them all. Let the whole world know about My love, and how easy it is to have an intimate relationship with Me. That's your commission. I will continue to pour into you greater understanding. The time is near for the book to be finished. I have great plans for the book. Do not be afraid to try new things. Change is coming to all. All of heaven is watching with anticipation of what is coming next. Only I know the plans I have for you. Many in heaven are living through you because they did not allow themselves to be used while on earth. We all want to see you fulfill your destiny written on the scrolls in heaven. Keep up the good work! Do not ever stop! I have given you the tenacity to make it."

Shirley's morning soaking time: Dear precious child, you were wondering about My anointed minister, but I answered your question as you were talking to your husband. I need you to keep going. Keep believing in My grace and My extravagant love for you all, and you will be able to fulfill your destinies. Just like My Word says, 'My love is everlasting and relentless.' I want to shower you all with My love and grace. There is no love on earth that comes close to Mine. Believe for the impossible because I can and will do it! My love and grace are immeasurable. You all have been through some hard attacks from the enemy. But you have come out as strong as ever and wiser than before. More revelations are coming to this team. So keep looking for them. You are still on the right track to fulfill your destinies. The encounters with Me and the angels are going to bring you such joy. You will be in awe with what I have in store for this team. This is the now time: time for My glory to shine! Arise and shine, for My glory has risen upon you! Remember that My words bring you peace and joy, My beloved. I love you, My daughter. Love, Papa."

In the evening, Stephanie and Shirley started marching around the living room table, playing praise music and reading aloud Revelation 4:1-2. In a few minutes, Mark saw four bright angels enter the room. The bright angels began shooting rainbow balls at them. Lightning bolts came down, then fireflies appeared. Observing from a heavenly portal, the Lion of Judah suddenly appeared with a tear in his eye. They invited him to come down. The lion walked around the room for a few minutes. Then the lion laid down in front of the big picture window, watching. They heard a loud "dong" sound as if someone had rung a large bell.

They invited Jesus to come dance and commune with them. Then He appeared in the portal and came dancing into the room! A huge angel, standing at the top of the portal, dropped a bundle of spiritual gifts down. In the portal were also many faces of the cloud of witnesses.

A sweet fragrance and a cool breeze manifested to all of them. Jesus began snapping His fingers to the praise music and swaying back and forth. For a little while longer, they continued to dance and to make declarations as they were prompted by Holy Spirit. (Holy Spirit had appeared as a big purple cloud hovering over the room until He filled the entire room.)

A great peace and a loving presence seemed to settle over them. At this point, they sat down to bask in God's Presence with no words to say.

April 7th

In the morning, Stephanie, Shirley, and Mark were visiting in the living room, sharing about the night before. As Shirley began reading a prophetic word from Facebook, Mark noticed something in the spirit realm.

As he looked over at the sofa, an orb of light appeared between Stephanie and Shirley. Mark had a "knowing" that the light orb was recording what Shirley was reading. The orb would enlarge when certain words were said. When they said "Jesus," the orb got larger.

Mark's eyes started burning, and then he noticed water and a face on the inside of the orb. The light orb moved over to Mark's hand, floating above it. God told Stephanie that this orb was an angel named Benjamin.

Mark placed his hands over his burning eyes. A vision appeared of two mountains with a beautiful blue river running between and through the mountains. The water was symbolic of the glory of God. Habakkuk 2:14 (ERV) says, "Then people everywhere will know about the Glory of the Lord. This news will spread just as water spreads out into the sea."

Shirley's morning soaking time: "It is time; the long-awaited time has come. It is your party time! You have been patiently waiting. Thank you for waiting on My *kairos* time and not jumping ahead of Me. Prosperity time is here. Your dreams are coming true. It is My good pleasure to give you the kingdom. Are you ready to ride the waves of My glory? It is wild and exciting and fun where My blessings abound abundantly! I don't miss a thing. I know the desires of your heart, and I pay attention to all the little details. It is My specialty. Forge ahead into your destinies, My mighty warriors! I have made you mighty on the earth. Shine forth in My glory! Stay humble, and remember how much I love you, My beloveds. I speak through whomever I want, especially those who are willing. That demon of guilt and condemnation (that came through religious doctrines) has been bound up, and you all are free from it now. Don't let any other religious demon come back. He had grown strong and big through the generations, but zap-bam went to the enemy last night through the Hosts of Heaven as your praise went forth!

Stephanie's morning soaking time, sitting in Father's lap: "I have so much to say. It excited Me to share My plans for you. You have transitioned to another phase. We are now cooking with oil. The cheers in heaven vibrated heaven last night when the demon was captured. He was taken to a dry place to torture no more. You tried something different than before. Remember to try new things and not get stuck in a rut. Change is good! You are experiencing heaven on earth. This is the way we rule and reign with Christ. Isn't it fun? The power that comes with faith, praise, and agreement is mind-blowing. Doors are closing, and I am opening new doors to walk through even as I speak. When you march around the table tonight, imagine yourself walking through the new door. You will really be doing this in the spirit realm. Physically close the door behind you. As you do this, the spirit realm will react. Gifting will continue to grow for all of you, even your children. They will fall in behind you. Tonight is going to be amazing! Remember that all of heaven is watching and decreeing over you! I am so pleased with this team. Mark witnessed the tear from My eye last night. The tear was not because I was sad. It's completely the opposite. Your heart brings tears to My eyes. You all make Me so happy! You do all of this for Me without seeing Me. The sight will soon increase for you and Shirley. There is so much power when you march in faith, more power than marching with spiritual sight. You ask, 'When will I get to see more in the spirit realm?' This has nothing to do with what you are doing or not doing. I have not allowed your eyes to see everything because the power that comes with your faith is needed at this time. Your time to see clearly is close at hand. I love you dearly—to the moon and back. Nothing could ever change that! Hugs and kisses, your Daddy."

In the evening, Shirley and Stephanie began the march around the coffee table, playing praise music and making decrees. Rainbow-colored angels started coming into the room. Holy Spirit came in as a purple cloud. They asked for the rainbow-colored balls that they had encountered the night before, but Mark said that blue balls were being shot out.

Suddenly a big, arched door appeared in the living room to the left of the coffee table. Mark could see turquoise blue water in the background. Five or six saints from the cloud of witnesses walked through the arched door, wearing casual attire.

Shirley began reading Revelation 4:1–2. Saints were looking down through the heavenly portal. An angel then appeared at the arched door, dancing to the music. Mark said, "Follow the angel through the door." So Stephanie and Shirley walked through the door by faith. Mark got up from the recliner and physically walked through the door also. He said that the Lion of Judah was right behind him. Then the door was shut. Shirley and Stephanie began the march again, and angels and the Lion of Judah joined them. Then, two men in a canoe appeared before Mark. One of them had red hair. A woman with reddish–blonde hair appeared next.

From the portal above, angels were throwing clear balls of light. Next, a shepherd holding a staff in his hand appeared. Upon seeing the shepherd, they began reciting Psalms 23. Swirls of pink color turned to blue.

Then, Jesus appeared sitting on a rock, looking into the water. Angels with white wings were coming into the room. They thanked Jesus for His glory and His love. Two angels walked straight through the living room and out, carrying a heavy, blue sapphire. To the left, emeralds were raining down in the spirit realm.

Next, Mark saw Jesus hugging someone in heaven. They all felt such love and peace at that moment in the encounter. Stephanie and Shirley sat down, feeling a tingling sensation through their bodies. They all relaxed in His Presence. All glory to God!

April 8th

Shirley's morning soaking time: "My dear daughter, I love how you put the pieces of the puzzle together. It is fun for us to watch you all receive the revelations. Yes, you all received the Apostle Paul's mantle. Great revelations are coming to this team—revelations that others do not yet know. Don't be afraid to write about and release what I have shown you all. It is needed to set the captives free from strongholds and the demons that get attached to the strongholds. You all are like Moses and what I did through him when I said, 'Let My people go.' I want them free! Just let yourselves be led by Me. Follow the promptings I put in your hearts and minds. No worries! I will say, 'This is the way. Walk in it.' Remember it is a new time for you. I am doing things in a new way. Forget the past—yours and that of the other members of your family. I've got this all figured out. So, no figuring is needed on your end. Go with My flow! It is easy when you do! Remember how relaxed and peaceful you felt when you stepped into the *new* last night, the brand-new door that was opened to you all. Let Me take care of everything. Yield to Me, and I will blow your minds with all the blessings and rewards I have for you all! Remember that My love is greater than being right. My dear daughter, My love for you will never fail you. You can depend on My love to get you through to your destiny. When you start reasoning in your mind, then doubting will come. That is when you are not meditating and trusting in My love for you. Live in the present. Do not even look back at the precious memories of the past because you are in this new time! It is a daily choice to let go of the past to live in the *new*. Ask for My grace to live in the new. It is free for the asking! You haven't gone this way before, so you will need Me to guide you. And it is My pleasure to give you the blessings of the kingdom. Remember that you are royalty, My beloved daughter. Love, Papa."

Stephanie's soaking time: "This is the year where dreams do come true, so dream big and watch Me show off! No dream is too big or impossible for Me! Watch, and you will see. Heaven on earth is My plan for you. Remember that dreams do come true! I have a future for you that you cannot comprehend. It is exciting and fun! When you see it, you will hop, skip, and run! My promises I am making to you today are true and will continue until your journey on earth is through. You are My precious child. Get ready! This ride is going to be wild!"

April 14ᵗʰ

God's message to His children: "The time you spend with Me is so powerful. I can reveal things to you—things that will help and direct your steps. Will you let Me do that in your life? I want and need you to spend time with Me daily. I have great plans for your future, and I long to share it with you. I can only use you if you choose to make yourself available to Me. I promise you a future of adventure and excitement. So many of My children go throughout their day and never even acknowledge My existence. I am here! Your Father, Savior, friend, and provider of all things. I can be much more to you if you will let Me. I need willing vessels to work through in this time on earth. This is a time for Me to reveal My power and to get My children focused on the good things, focused on their true purpose. My plans for you are better than you can imagine for yourself. Give Me a chance to show you. I am always willing and ready to spend time with you. I love you, your true Father."

April 15ᵗʰ

Stephanie's soaking time: "I love you so much. You are the apple of My eye. You please Me. I smile down on you with great joy. Continue to pray over your family. The enemy looks for any opportunity to steal, kill, and destroy. I have amazing plans for this family. Let Me direct you in My ways. Continue to spend time with Me. Be open to what I want to show you. I encourage you to look for Me throughout your day. Finish the book. The book is the key to moving forward in this time. Confide in Me with your desires. I am your Father, and I delight in providing for My children."

April 18th

God's message to His children: "I want the best for the United States. This country's foundation is based on My principles. I need America to be strong. I do not have and neither will I ever have plans to destroy this precious nation. When I look at her, I see promise and success. She is and will always be special to Me. I have used her and will continue to use her to spread the great news of My Son. Rest assured that America has yet to see her best days!"

April 21st

Shirley's morning soaking time, sitting in Papa's lap: "My dear precious child, I love your faith in Me. I don't have many that have this kind of faith because of religious demons and strongholds. Keep coming to Me, and all your dreams will be a reality in your life. I so yearn to bless My children, but most have not allowed Me to do so. Will you let Me, My beloved daughter? I am your love, and Love loves to give. No holding back from My children. There has been a great disconnect between Me and My children for so long, but you have said, 'Not my will, but Your will, Your way, Papa.' This choice has opened the door for Me to do wonderful and amazing things in you, for you, and through you. This is the Master Key. Just like Jesus did, you do. It is necessary. I need your cooperation, your agreement with Me. But wow! Glory to Me be when one of My children will submit to My will and My ways! It can change the world! What a powerful team when you allow Me to do it My way! I love you, My darling. Remember My heart toward you. Love, your Papa forever."

Stephanie's morning soaking time: "I have many surprises for you. I love surprising you. You make Me laugh with your excitement and childlike faith. We are ecstatic here in heaven that you are once again together! There is power in numbers. I have a special ceremony planned for tonight. Do as you usually do with praise and marching; then the ceremony will begin. Do as Holy Spirit leads. Mark will be able to see more clearly. All of heaven is getting ready for the ceremony. Dress nice. Soon the book will be ready. When it is finished, I want you to come together, and I will commission the book. I will direct you on the cover of the book just as I have done with other things. I am so pleased with you. I love hearing you discuss My plans and the revelations given to you. Your faith allows Me to do more in your lives. I can use that kind of faith to do more than imagined. When you don't put limitations on Me, then heaven is the limit. I declare that there are no limits on this team! You can do anything through Me."

In the evening, Stephanie and Shirley marched around the living room table, imagining themselves dressed in beautiful ball gowns. Mark pictured himself in king's attire with a robe for the ceremony.

Angels began flooding the room. Jesus appeared, wearing a white gown with a purple robe. He gave each of them a hug, then began dancing with them. Shirley heard that Jesus was going to crown them. They were caught up in the spirit to a grand ballroom in heaven. Mark watched as Jesus crowned Shirley, Stephanie, and then himself.

The dancing started again. Mark heard that all of them were to be seated in the royal chairs. Jesus sat down among them, making a toast. While they were seated, Apostle Paul prophesied over them and blessed them. The scene changed to the three of them seated at the end of a long table eating dinner with Jesus and the cloud of witnesses.

After dinner, they found themselves in a heavenly garden, walking over an arched bridge with Father and Jesus. Father shared His loving heart with them.

The above encounter was confirmed by a seer the next day. The seer wasn't present at the time, and he was not given any clues. In the spirit, the seer saw crowns on their heads and described them in detail just as Mark had seen the night before. He said they were the first to receive the crowns during this time, and there were more people coming after them; their ball gowns and king's attire were hung in their heavenly mansions, but they continued wearing the crowns, and their crowns were visible to all the spirit realm.

April 24th

Shirley dreamed last night that God wanted a salvation prayer in the book.

May 4th

Stephanie's soaking time: "I am your provider, confidant, protector, Savior, and friend. You mean the world to Me. There is nothing that could change that. There is a place in My heart for all who come to Me. My grace is enough for any situation. There is nothing My blood can't cover. I am so pleased with you and Shirley. You understand how easy a relationship with Me truly is. I require very little. If My children would take a baby step toward Me, I would do the rest. Tell them! Please tell them. My love is easy!"

May 8th

Shirley's soaking time: Shirley went into a trance. In the trance, she saw Jesus in a flowing robe, holding her as a young child in His loving arms. Then the scene changed into a bucket of water being poured out all over the ground. Shirley asked Holy Spirit, "What does this mean? What are you showing me?" Holy Spirit answered, "The bucket of water is My glory being poured out on this earth. Be a bucket full of My glory and pour it out on others. Let My glory that is in you and on you splash on those that I bring to you. Rivers of living water will flow out of this team. It starts out in you as buckets, then it expands and increases into mighty rivers of living water—My river of glory. Let My river flow through you. Rest in the river of My love and glory. Remember My glory is a rest for you from all your works and religion. Let My glory river flow—it cannot be dammed up. It is going to flood this earth! My kingdom come, My will be done on this earth as it is in heaven. It is glory time, kingdom time. Rule and reign with Me, My beloved queen—you have been crowned. Make those decrees! No turning back! March forward! Run your glory race! All glory comes from Me! You already have My power in you, so release it! Give it out. I will bring the divine appointments to you. I have so much planned—fun and awesome events. I love you, dear daughter. Hugs and kisses, Holy Spirit."

May 10th

Stephanie and Shirley were standing together with their families, making decrees, saying, "Our hands are weapons. We are superheroes, and at the wave of our hands, supernatural power comes out of them." Suddenly, Jesus appeared with a vial of oil in His hands. They each held out their hands for Jesus to anoint them with the oil. Jesus said, "Rub it in." Wow! Glory to God!

May 11th

Stephanie's soaking time: "I love you and want the best life possible for you. It can all be yours if you will just believe. It is that easy! My children make it harder than it should be. Don't you want the best for your child? That is the same for Me, your Father. I have no limitations on what I can and will do for you. You determine My limitations. It's all what you believe. If you believe I can do all things, then all things are available to you. Declare and decree what you need and want. Your words are powerful! I need you to step into this new way of thinking. You will need to believe in your power as My child to do what I have called you to do. You are royalty. The King of all Kings says so!"

May 12th

Shirley's morning soaking time: "My dear daughter, I am so proud of you all. You all are believing, declaring, and receiving. I finally get to bless some of My children. We have longed to bless My children abundantly but have been unable due to doubt and unbelief. Remember the chariot ride tonight! I have it all planned out for you. Do you like My plans so far? I have fun doing this for this team." Shirley answered, "Yes, Papa, Jesus, and Holy Spirit. I must confess, though, that it has been a little hard in the waiting." Papa said, "I have had to give you the downloads and the confirmations a little at a time. I knew it would be overwhelming to the team to receive too much too soon. I know the exact time for everything to come into manifestation on earth. So keep on trusting Me and letting Me lead you as I have been doing. Your faith has been stretched today. And you all did great! Good job, My children! What a joy you all are to Me, Jesus, and Holy Spirit! Now take your chariot ride! There is no time like the present. Have you liked all My presents? I love you, My daughter, and I love that you love My Presence. I love yours, too. Hugs and kisses, sweet daughter of Mine. Your Papa."

In the evening, Shirley and Stephanie marched around a coffee table in the vacation condo, making decrees and playing praise songs. The two seers were present, anticipating the supernatural. After a few minutes, they asked for the chariot to come, and it came into the living room of the condo. Shirley and Stephanie went over to the spiritual door (pointed out by one of the seers as to the location) and stepped in by faith. The seer also stepped in. Suddenly, the three of them felt wind blowing on their faces. (The air conditioner or ceiling fan was not on.) The seer told them the moment they arrived at the throne room in heaven. They walked over to Father, who was sitting on His throne. Jesus was to the right of Him. They sat down on Their laps, and communed with Them, thanking Them for the chariot ride, Their love, and Their Presence.

May 25th

Shirley's soaking time: At first, Shirley was sitting in Papa's lap as a little child. Then Shirley walked over to Jesus. An outdoor shower appeared with a pink curtain. Shirley asked Jesus if He wanted her to step in. Jesus replied, "Yes." So Shirley stepped in, and Jesus infused His light and His glory, showering her with His love. After a few minutes, Shirley asked if it was time to step out. Jesus said, "Twirl around." As Shirley obeyed, she was instantly a young woman wearing a white gown. Jesus continued, "Step out, My bride. Step out, for you have all of Me in you wherever you go. Go into all the world, knowing that you have all of Me—all My power, My love, My glory, and My grace. Everything you need to impact the world for My kingdom. Go and release who I am to the world!"

May 28th

Shirley's soaking time: Shirley went into a trance. She was a little girl in heaven, sitting on a long table with her legs dangling off. All of heaven was getting ready for a feast. A big celebration was taking place in honor of all the veterans and those serving in the military.

June 3rd

Shirley's soaking time, sitting in Papa's lap: "My sweet daughter, you are precious. Most of My children do not have Me as their first love. They are deceived. They think they do, but they are not yet there in their hearts. They don't even know how to access My throne without going through certain rituals. No worries, My child! Keep on coming to Me, and I'll show you even more. Your destiny is great, My child. Most of My children do not fulfill their destinies because they do not come to Me or even know how. This book is vital for My children. They need to know how easy it is to come to Me, how loving I am, and how much I yearn to have fellowship with each one of My children."

June 14th

God's message to His children: "What I am doing is new. The revelations in the book are new to so many. My children are hungry for the truth. The book will set them free! Free for Me to move in and through them like the world has never seen before. The plans I have for My children are perfect. Keep your eyes on My Son, Jesus, and you will avoid the snares of the enemy. You were made for such a time as this!"

June 26th

Early in the morning, Stephanie was singing praise and worship songs to the Father, Jesus, and Holy Spirit, and she found herself in the throne room dancing with Jesus. He loves to dance. She spent time singing individually to Jesus, Holy Spirit, and Father God. She jumped into Father's lap, and He lovingly gave her a big hug. In the natural, she could feel His arms wrap around her, holding her tight. The sense of love, peace, and happiness was amazing!

The Commissioning of This Book

On July 15, 2018, the team attended church. The apostle, a prophetic team, and other church members prayed over and blessed the book. Several people gave prophetic words: "God will heal souls through the words He gave you; generations will know His name and be healed by His words; this book will be a bestseller; it will go to the nations; it needs to be written in multiple languages; and God wants a sequel to this book—He is releasing a hunger on this earth, and it will have His children hungry for Him."

CPSIA information can be obtained
at www.ICGtesting.com
Printed in the USA
LVHW031328261118
598271LV00005B/296/P

9 781545 645475